ON IDEOLOGY

RADICAL THINKERS }V

SET 1 ($12/£6/$14CAN)

MINIMA MORALIA
Reflections on a Damaged Life
THEODOR ADORNO
ISBN-13: 978 1 84467 051 2

FOR MARX
LOUIS ALTHUSSER
ISBN-13: 978 1 84467 052 9

THE SYSTEM OF OBJECTS
JEAN BAUDRILLARD
ISBN-13: 978 1 84467 053 6

LIBERALISM AND DEMOCRACY
NORBERTO BOBBIO
ISBN-13: 978 1 84467 062 8

THE POLITICS OF FRIENDSHIP
JACQUES DERRIDA
ISBN-13: 978 1 84467 054 3

THE FUNCTION OF CRITICISM
TERRY EAGLETON
ISBN-13: 978 1 84467 055 0

SIGNS TAKEN FOR WONDERS
On the Sociology of Literary Forms
FRANCO MORETTI
ISBN-13: 978 1 84467 056 7

THE RETURN OF THE POLITICAL
CHANTAL MOUFFE
ISBN-13: 978 1 84467 057 4

SEXUALITY IN THE FIELD OF VISION
JACQUELINE ROSE
ISBN-13: 978 1 84467 058 1

THE INFORMATION BOMB
PAUL VIRILIO
ISBN-13: 978 1 84467 059 8

CULTURE AND MATERIALISM
RAYMOND WILLIAMS
ISBN-13: 978 1 84467 060 4

THE METASTASES OF ENJOYMENT
On Women and Causality
SLAVOJ ŽIŽEK
ISBN-13: 978 1 84467 061 1

SET 2 ($12.95/£6.99/$17CAN)

AESTHETICS AND POLITICS
THEODOR ADORNO, WALTER BENJAMIN, ERNST BLOCH, BERTOLT BRECHT, GEORG LUKÁCS
ISBN-13: 978 1 84467 570 8

INFANCY AND HISTORY
On the Destruction of Experience
GIORGIO AGAMBEN
ISBN-13: 978 1 84467 571 5

POLITICS AND HISTORY
Montesquieu, Rousseau, Marx
LOUIS ALTHUSSER
ISBN-13: 978 1 84467 572 2

FRAGMENTS
JEAN BAUDRILLARD
ISBN-13: 978 1 84467 573 9

LOGICS OF DISINTEGRATION
Poststructuralist Thought and the Claims of Critical Theory
PETER DEWS
ISBN-13: 978 1 84467 574 6

LATE MARXISM
Adorno, Or, The Persistence of the Dialectic
FREDRIC JAMESON
ISBN-13: 978 1 84467 575 3

EMANCIPATION(S)
ERNESTO LACLAU
ISBN-13: 978 1 84467 576 0

THE POLITICAL DESCARTES
Reason, Ideology and the Bourgeois Project
ANTONIO NEGRI
ISBN-13: 978 1 84467 582 1

ON THE SHORES OF POLITICS
JACQUES RANCIÈRE
ISBN-13: 978 1 84467 577 7

STRATEGY OF DECEPTION
PAUL VIRILIO
ISBN-13: 978 1 84467 578 4

POLITICS OF MODERNISM
Against the New Conformists
RAYMOND WILLIAMS
ISBN-13: 978 1 84467 580 7

THE INDIVISIBLE REMAINDER
On Schelling and Related Matters
SLAVOJ ŽIŽEK
ISBN-13: 978 1 84467 581 4

ON IDEOLOGY

Louis Althusser

VERSO

London • New York

First published by New Left Books 1971
Copyright © New Left Books 1971, 1976
This edition published by Verso 2008
Copyright © Verso 2008
'Ideology and Ideological State Apparatuses' first published in *La Pensée*
1970 (copyright © *La Pensée* 1970); 'Reply to John Lewis' first published in
Marxism Today, October–November 1972, rewritten, expanded and repub-
lished as *Réponse a John Lewis* by François Maspero 1973 (copyright ©
Louis Althusser 1973); 'Freud and Lacan' first published in *La Nouvelle
Critique* 1964 (copyright © *La Nouvelle Critique* 1964), translation
copyright © New Left Review 1969; 'A Letter on Art in Reply to André
Daspre' first published in *La Nouvelle Critique* 1966
(copyright © *La Nouvelle Critique* 1966).

1 3 5 7 9 10 8 6 4 2

Verso
UK: 6 Meard Street, London W1F 0EG
USA: 180 Varick Street, New York, NY 10014-4606
www.versobooks.com

Verso is the imprint of New Left Books

ISBN-13: 978-1-84467-202-8

British Library Cataloguing in Publication Data
A catalogue record for this book is available from the British Library

Library of Congress Cataloging-in-Publication Data
A catalog record for this book is available from the Library of Congress

Printed and bound by ScandBook AB, Sweden

Contents

Ideology and Ideological State Apparatuses (Notes towards an Investigation)

ON THE REPRODUCTION OF THE CONDITIONS OF PRODUCTION[1]

I must now expose more fully something which was briefly glimpsed in my analysis when I spoke of the necessity to renew the means of production if production is to be possible. That was a passing hint. Now I shall consider it for itself.

As Marx said, every child knows that a social formation which did not reproduce the conditions of production at the same time as it produced would not last a year.[2] The ultimate condition of production is therefore the reproduction of the conditions of production. This may be 'simple' (reproducing exactly the previous conditions of production) or 'on an extended scale' (expanding them). Let us ignore this last distinction for the moment.

What, then, is *the reproduction of the conditions of production?*

Here we are entering a domain which is both very fam-

1. This text is made up of two extracts from an ongoing study. The sub-title 'Notes towards an Investigation' is the author's own. The ideas expounded should not be regarded as more than the introduction to a discussion.
2. Marx to Kugelmann, 11 July 1868, *Selected Correspondence*, Moscow, 1955, p. 209.

iliar (since *Capital* Volume Two) and uniquely ignored. The tenacious obviousnesses (ideological obviousnesses of an empiricist type) of the point of view of production alone, or even of that of mere productive practice (itself abstract in relation to the process of production) are so integrated into our everyday 'consciousness' that it is extremely hard, not to say almost impossible, to raise oneself to the *point of view of reproduction*. Nevertheless, everything outside this point of view remains abstract (worse than one-sided: distorted) – even at the level of production, and, *a fortiori*, at that of mere practice.

Let us try and examine the matter methodically.

To simplify my exposition, and assuming that every social formation arises from a dominant mode of production, I can say that the process of production sets to work the existing productive forces in and under definite relations of production.

It follows that, in order to exist, every social formation must reproduce the conditions of its production at the same time as it produces, and in order to be able to produce. It must therefore reproduce:

1. the productive forces,
2. the existing relations of production.

Reproduction of the Means of Production

Everyone (including the bourgeois economists whose work is national accounting, or the modern 'macro-economic' 'theoreticians') now recognizes, because Marx compellingly proved it in *Capital* Volume Two, that no production is possible which does not allow for the reproduction of the material conditions of production: the reproduction of the means of production.

The average economist, who is no different in this than

the average capitalist, knows that each year it is essential to foresee what is needed to replace what has been used up or worn out in production: raw material, fixed installations (buildings), instruments of production (machines), etc. I say the average economist = the average capitalist, for they both express the point of view of the firm, regarding it as sufficient simply to give a commentary on the terms of the firm's financial accounting practice.

But thanks to the genius of Quesnay who first posed this 'glaring' problem, and to the genius of Marx who resolved it, we know that the reproduction of the material conditions of production cannot be thought at the level of the firm, because it does not exist at that level in its real conditions. What happens at the level of the firm is an effect, which only gives an idea of the necessity of reproduction, but absolutely fails to allow its conditions and mechanisms to be thought.

A moment's reflection is enough to be convinced of this: Mr X, a capitalist who produces woollen yarn in his spinning-mill, has to 'reproduce' his raw material, his machines, etc. But *he* does not produce them for his own production – other capitalists do: an Australian sheep-farmer, Mr Y, a heavy engineer producing machine-tools, Mr Z, etc., etc. And Mr Y and Mr Z, in order to produce those products which are the condition of the reproduction of Mr X's conditions of production, also have to reproduce the conditions of their own production, and so on to infinity – the whole in proportions such that, on the national and even the world market, the demand for means of production (for reproduction) can be satisfied by the supply.

In order to think this mechanism, which leads to a kind of 'endless chain', it is necessary to follow Marx's 'global' procedure, and to study in particular the relations of the circulation of capital between Department I (production of means of production) and Department II (production of means of consumption), and the realization of surplus-value, in *Capital*, Volumes Two and Three.

We shall not go into the analysis of this question. It is enough to have mentioned the existence of the necessity of the reproduction of the material conditions of production.

Reproduction of Labour-Power

However, the reader will not have failed to note one thing. We have discussed the reproduction of the means of production – but not the reproduction of the productive forces. We have therefore ignored the reproduction of what distinguishes the productive forces from the means of production, i.e. the reproduction of labour power.

From the observation of what takes place in the firm, in particular from the examination of the financial accounting practice which predicts amortization and investment, we have been able to obtain an approximate idea of the existence of the material process of reproduction, but we are now entering a domain in which the observation of what happens in the firm is, if not totally blind, at least almost entirely so, and for good reason: the reproduction of labour power takes place essentially outside the firm.

How is the reproduction of labour power ensured?

It is ensured by giving labour power the material means with which to reproduce itself: by wages. Wages feature in the accounting of each enterprise, but as 'wage capital',[3] not at all as a condition of the material reproduction of labour power.

However, that is in fact how it 'works', since wages represents only that part of the value produced by the expendi-

---

3. Marx gave it its scientific concept: *variable capital.*

ture of labour power which is indispensable for its reproduction: sc. indispensable to the reconstitution of the labour power of the wage-earner (the wherewithal to pay for housing, food and clothing, in short to enable the wage-earner to present himself again at the factory gate the next day – and every further day God grants him); and we should add: indispensable for raising and educating the children in whom the proletarian reproduces himself (in n models where n = o, 1, 2, etc. . . .) as labour power.

Remember that this quantity of value (wages) necessary for the reproduction of labour power is determined not by the needs of a 'biological' Guaranteed Minimum Wage (*Salaire Minimum Interprofessionnel Garanti*) alone, but by the needs of a historical minimum (Marx noted that English workers need beer while French proletarians need wine) – i.e. a historically variable minimum.

I should also like to point out that this minimum is doubly historical in that it is not defined by the historical needs of the working class 'recognized' by the capitalist class, but by the historical needs imposed by the proletarian class struggle (a double class struggle: against the lengthening of the working day and against the reduction of wages).

However, it is not enough to ensure for labour power the material conditions of its reproduction if it is to be reproduced as labour power. I have said that the available labour power must be 'competent', i.e. suitable to be set to work in the complex system of the process of production. The development of the productive forces and the type of unity historically constitutive of the productive forces at a given moment produce the result that the labour power has to be (diversely) skilled and therefore reproduced as such. Diversely: according to the requirements of the socio-technical division of labour, its different 'jobs' and 'posts'.

How is this reproduction of the (diversified) skills of

labour power provided for in a capitalist regime? Here, unlike social formations characterized by slavery or serfdom, this reproduction of the skills of labour power tends (this is a tendential law) decreasingly to be provided for 'on the spot' (apprenticeship within production itself), but is achieved more and more outside production: by the capitalist education system, and by other instances and institutions.

What do children learn at school? They go varying distances in their studies, but at any rate they learn to read, to write and to add – i.e. a number of techniques, and a number of other things as well, including elements (which may be rudimentary or on the contrary thoroughgoing) of 'scientific' or 'literary culture', which are directly useful in the different jobs in production (one instruction for manual workers, another for technicians, a third for engineers, a final one for higher management, etc.). Thus they learn 'know-how'.

But besides these techniques and knowledges, and in learning them, children at school also learn the 'rules' of good behaviour, i.e. the attitude that should be observed by every agent in the division of labour, according to the job he is 'destined' for: rules of morality, civic and professional conscience, which actually means rules of respect for the socio-technical division of labour and ultimately the rules of the order established by class domination. They also learn to 'speak proper French', to 'handle' the workers correctly, i.e. actually (for the future capitalists and their servants) to 'order them about' properly, i.e. (ideally) to 'speak to them' in the right way, etc.

To put this more scientifically, I shall say that the reproduction of labour power requires not only a reproduction of its skills, but also, at the same time, a reproduction of its submission to the rules of the established order, i.e. a reproduction of submission to the ruling ideology for the *reproduction of labor also includes training people in their relationship to ideology.*

workers, and a reproduction of the ability to manipulate <u>the ruling ideology correctly for the agents of exploitation</u> <u>and repression, so that they, too, will provide for the dom-</u> ination of the ruling class 'in words'.

In other words, the school (but also other State institutions like the Church, or other apparatuses like the Army) teaches 'know-how', but in forms which ensure *subjection to the ruling ideology* or the mastery of its 'practice'. All the agents of production, exploitation and repression, not to speak of the 'professionals of ideology' (Marx), must in one way or another be 'steeped' in this ideology in order to perform their tasks 'conscientiously' – the tasks of the exploited (the proletarians), of the exploiters (the capitalists), of the exploiters' auxiliaries (the managers), or of the high priests of the ruling ideology (its 'functionaries'), etc.

The reproduction of labour power thus reveals as its *sine qua non* not only the reproduction of its 'skills' but also the reproduction of its subjection to the ruling ideology or of the 'practice' of that ideology, with the proviso that it is not enough to say 'not only but also', for it is clear that *it is in the forms and under the forms of ideological subjection that provision is made for the reproduction of the skills of labour power*.

But this is to recognize the effective presence of a new reality: *ideology*.

Here I shall make two comments.

The first is to round off my analysis of reproduction.

I have just given a rapid survey of the forms of the reproduction of the productive forces, i.e. of the means of production on the one hand, and of labour power on the other.

But I have not yet approached the question of the *reproduction of the relations of production*. This is a *crucial question* for the Marxist theory of the mode of production.

To let it pass would be a theoretical omission – worse, a serious political error.

I shall therefore discuss it. But in order to obtain the means to discuss it, I shall have to make another long detour.

The second comment is that in order to make this detour, I am obliged to re-raise my old question: what is a society?

INFRASTRUCTURE AND SUPERSTRUCTURE

On a number of occasions[4] I have insisted on the revolutionary character of the Marxist conception of the 'social whole' insofar as it is distinct from the Hegelian 'totality'. I said (and this thesis only repeats famous propositions of historical materialism) that Marx conceived the structure of every society as constituted by 'levels' or 'instances' articulated by a specific determination: the *infrastructure*, or economic base (the 'unity' of the productive forces and the relations of production) and the *superstructure*, which itself contains two 'levels' or 'instances': the politico-legal (law and the State) and ideology (the different ideologies, religious, ethical, legal, political, etc.).

Besides its theoretico-didactic interest (it reveals the difference between Marx and Hegel), this representation has the following crucial theoretical advantage: it makes it possible to inscribe in the theoretical apparatus of its essential concepts what I have called their *respective indices of effectivity*. What does this mean?

It is easy to see that this representation of the structure of every society as an edifice containing a base (infrastruc-

4. In *For Marx* and *Reading Capital*, 1965 (English editions 1969 and 1970 respectively).

[handwritten note: If diff. between Althusser & Williams is abt humanism, does this mean we need "humans" for mobile fluid "base" or "culture"?]

... e two 'floors' of the super- ... quite precise, a spatial meta- ... raphy (*topique*).[5] Like every ... sts something, makes some- thing visible. What? Precisely this: that the upper floors could not 'stay up' (in the air) alone, if they did not rest precisely on their base.

Thus the object of the metaphor of the edifice is to represent above all the 'determination in the last instance' by the economic base. The effect of this spatial metaphor is to endow the base with an index of effectivity known by the famous terms: the determination in the last instance of what happens in the upper 'floors' (of the superstructure) by what happens in the economic base.

Given this index of effectivity 'in the last instance', the 'floors' of the superstructure are clearly endowed with different indices of effectivity. What kind of indices?

It is possible to say that the floors of the superstructure are not determinant in the last instance, but that they are determined by the effectivity of the base; that if they are determinant in their own (as yet undefined) ways, this is true only insofar as they are determined by the base.

Their index of effectivity (or determination), as determined by the determination in the last instance of the base, is thought by the Marxist tradition in two ways: (1) there is a 'relative autonomy' of the superstructure with respect to the base; (2) there is a 'reciprocal action' of the superstructure on the base.

We can therefore say that the great theoretical advantage of the Marxist topography, i.e. of the spatial metaphor of

5. *Topography* from the Greek *topos*: place. A topography represents in a definite space the respective *sites* occupied by several realities: thus the economic is *at the bottom* (the base), the superstructure *above it*.

the edifice (base and superstructure) is simultaneously that it reveals that questions of determination (or of index of effectivity) are crucial; that it reveals that it is the base which in the last instance determines the whole edifice; and that, as a consequence, it obliges us to pose the theoretical problem of the types of 'derivatory' effectivity peculiar to the superstructure, i.e. it obliges us to think what the Marxist tradition calls conjointly the relative autonomy of the superstructure and the reciprocal action of the superstructure on the base.

The greatest disadvantage of this representation of the structure of every society by the spatial metaphor of an edifice, is obviously the fact that it is metaphorical: i.e. it remains *descriptive*.

It now seems to me that it is possible and desirable to represent things differently (NB, I do not mean by this that I want to reject the classical metaphor, for that metaphor itself requires that we go beyond it. And I am not going beyond it in order to reject it as outworn. I simply want to attempt to think what it gives us in the form of a description.

I believe that it is possible and necessary to think what characterizes the essential of the existence and nature of the superstructure *on the basis of reproduction*. Once one takes the point of view of reproduction, many of the questions whose existence was indicated by the spatial metaphor of the edifice, but to which it could not give a conceptual answer, are immediately illuminated.

My basic thesis is that it is not possible to pose these questions (and therefore to answer them) *except from the point of view of reproduction*.

I shall give a short analysis of Law, the State and Ideology *from this point of view*. And I shall reveal what happens both from the point of view of practice and production on the one hand, and from that of reproduction on the other.

THE STATE

The Marxist tradition is strict, here: in the *Communist Manifesto* and the *Eighteenth Brumaire* (and in all the later classical texts, above all in Marx's writings on the Paris Commune and Lenin's on *State and Revolution*), the State is explicitly conceived as a repressive apparatus. The State is a 'machine' of repression, which enables the ruling classes (in the nineteenth century the bourgeois class and the 'class' of big landowners) to ensure their domination over the working class, thus enabling the former to subject the latter to the process of surplus-value extortion (i.e. to capitalist exploitation).

The State is thus first of all what the Marxist classics have called *the State apparatus*. This term means: not only the specialized apparatus (in the narrow sense) whose existence and necessity I have recognized in relation to the requirements of legal practice, i.e. the police, the courts, the prisons; but also the army, which (the proletariat has paid for this experience with its blood) intervenes directly as a supplementary repressive force in the last instance, when the police and its specialized auxiliary corps are 'outrun by events'; and above this ensemble, the head of State, the government and the administration.

Presented in this form, the Marxist-Leninist 'theory' of the State has its finger on the essential point, and not for one moment can there be any question of rejecting the fact that this really is the essential point. The State apparatus, which defines the State as a force of repressive execution and intervention 'in the interests of the ruling classes' in the class struggle conducted by the bourgeoisie and its allies against the proletariat, is quite certainly the State, and quite certainly defines its basic 'function'.

From Descriptive Theory to Theory as such

Nevertheless, here too, as I pointed out with respect to the metaphor of the edifice (infrastructure and superstructure), this presentation of the nature of the State is still partly descriptive.

As I shall often have occasion to use this adjective (descriptive), a word of explanation is necessary in order to remove any ambiguity.

Whenever, in speaking of the metaphor of the edifice or of the Marxist 'theory' of the State, I have said that these are descriptive conceptions or representations of their objects, I had no ulterior critical motives. On the contrary, I have every grounds to think that great scientific dis-coveries cannot help but pass through the phase of what I shall call *descriptive 'theory'*. This is the first phase of every theory, at least in the domain which concerns us (that of the science of social formations). As such, one might – and in my opinion one must – envisage this phase as a transitional one, necessary to the development of the theory. That it is transitional is inscribed in my expression: 'descriptive theory', which reveals in its conjunction of terms the equivalent of a kind of 'contradiction'. In fact, the term theory 'clashes' to some extent with the adjective 'descriptive' which I have attached to it. This means quite precisely: (1) that the 'descriptive theory' really is, without a shadow of a doubt, the irreversible beginning of the theory; but (2) that the 'descriptive' form in which the theory is presented requires, precisely as an effect of this 'contradiction', a development of the theory which goes beyond the form of 'description'.

Let me make this idea clearer by returning to our present object: the State.

When I say that the Marxist 'theory' of the State available to us is still partly 'descriptive', that means first and foremost that this descriptive 'theory' is without the shadow of a doubt precisely the beginning of the Marxist theory of the State, and that this beginning gives us the essential point, i.e. the decisive principle of every later development of the theory.

Indeed, I shall call the descriptive theory of the State correct, since it is perfectly possible to make the vast majority of the facts in the domain with which it is concerned correspond to the definition it gives of its object. Thus, the definition of the State as a class State, existing in the repressive State apparatus, casts a brilliant light on all the facts observable in the various orders of repression whatever their domains: from the massacres of June 1848 and of the Paris Commune, of Bloody Sunday, May 1905 in Petrograd, of the Resistance, of Charonne, etc., to the mere (and relatively anodyne) interventions of a 'censorship' which has banned Diderot's *La Réligieuse* or a play by Gatti on Franco; it casts light on all the direct or indirect forms of exploitation and extermination of the masses of the people (imperialist wars); it casts light on that subtle everyday domination beneath which can be glimpsed, in the forms of political democracy, for example, what Lenin, following Marx, called the dictatorship of the bourgeoisie.

And yet the descriptive theory of the State represents a phase in the constitution of the theory which itself demands the 'supersession' of this phase. For it is clear that if the definition in question really does give us the means to identify and recognize the facts of oppression by relating them to the State, conceived as the repressive State apparatus, this 'interrelationship' gives rise to a very special kind of obviousness, about which I shall have something to say in a moment: 'Yes, that's how it is, that's really true!'[6]

6. See p. 158 below, *On Ideology*.

And the accumulation of facts within the definition of the State may multiply examples, but it does not really advance the definition of the State, i.e. the scientific theory of the State. Every descriptive theory thus runs the risk of 'blocking' the development of the theory, and yet that development is essential.

That is why I think that, in order to develop this descriptive theory into theory as such, i.e. in order to understand further the mechanisms of the State in its functioning, I think that it is indispensable to *add* something to the classical definition of the State as a State apparatus.

The Essentials of the Marxist Theory of the State

Let me first clarify one important point: the State (and its existence in its apparatus) has no meaning except as a function of *State power*. The whole of the political class struggle revolves around the State. By which I mean around the possession, i.e. the seizure and conservation of State power by a certain class or by an alliance between classes or class fractions. This first clarification obliges me to distinguish between State power (conservation of State power or seizure of State power), the objective of the political class struggle on the one hand, and the State apparatus on the other.

We know that the State apparatus may survive, as is proved by bourgeois 'revolutions' in nineteenth-century France (1830, 1848), by *coups d'état* (2 December, May 1958), by collapses of the State (the fall of the Empire in 1870, of the Third Republic in 1940), or by the political rise of the petty bourgeoisie (1890–95 in France), etc., without the State apparatus being affected or modified: it may survive political events which affect the possession of State power.

Even after a social revolution like that of 1917, a large part of the State apparatus survived after the seizure of State power by the alliance of the proletariat and the small peasantry: Lenin repeated the fact again and again.

It is possible to describe the distinction between State power and State apparatus as part of the 'Marxist theory' of the State, explicitly present since Marx's *Eighteenth Brumaire* and *Class Struggles in France*.

To summarize the 'Marxist theory of the State' on this point, it can be said that the Marxist classics have always claimed that (1) the State is the repressive State apparatus, (2) State power and State apparatus must be distinguished, (3) the objective of the class struggle concerns State power, and in consequence the use of the State apparatus by the classes (or alliance of classes or of fractions of classes) holding State power as a function of their class objectives, and (4) the proletariat must seize State power in order to destroy the existing bourgeois State apparatus and, in a first phase, replace it with a quite different, proletarian, State apparatus, then in later phases set in motion a radical process, that of the destruction of the State (the end of State power, the end of every State apparatus).

In this perspective, therefore, what I would propose to add to the 'Marxist theory' of the State is already there in so many words. But it seems to me that even with this supplement, this theory is still in part descriptive, although it does now contain complex and differential elements whose functioning and action cannot be understood without recourse to further supplementary theoretical development.

The State Ideological Apparatuses

Thus, what has to be added to the 'Marxist theory' of the State is something else.

Here we must advance cautiously in a terrain which, in fact, the Marxist classics entered long before us, but without having systematized in theoretical form the decisive advances implied by their experiences and procedures. Their experiences and procedures were indeed restricted in the main to the terrain of political practice.

In fact, i.e. in their political practice, the Marxist classics treated the State as a more complex reality than the definition of it given in the 'Marxist theory of the State', even when it has been supplemented as I have just suggested. They recognized this complexity in their practice, but they did not express it in a corresponding theory.[7]

I should like to attempt a very schematic outline of this corresponding theory. To that end, I propose the following thesis.

In order to advance the theory of the State it is indispensable to take into account not only the distinction between *State power* and *State apparatus*, but also another reality which is clearly on the side of the (repressive) State apparatus, but must not be confused with it. I shall call this reality by its concept: *the ideological State apparatuses*.

What are the ideological State apparatuses (ISAs)?

They must not be confused with the (repressive) State apparatus. Remember that in Marxist theory, the State Apparatus (SA) contains: the Government, the Admin-

---

7. To my knowledge, Gramsci is the only one who went any distance in the road I am taking. He had the 'remarkable' idea that the State could not be reduced to the (Repressive) State Apparatus, but included, as he put it, a certain number of institutions from '*civil society*': the Church, the Schools, the trade unions, etc. Unfortunately, Gramsci did not systematize his institutions, which remained in the state of acute but fragmentary notes (cf. Gramsci, *Selections from the Prison Notebooks*, International Publishers, 1971, pp. 12, 259, 260–3; see also the letter to Tatiana Schucht, 7 September 1931, in *Lettre del Carcere*, Einaudi, 1968, p. 479. English-language translation in preparation.

Repressive State Apparatus

istration, the Army, the Police, the Courts, the Prisons, etc., which constitute what I shall in future call the Repressive State Apparatus. Repressive suggests that the State Apparatus in question 'functions by violence' – at least ultimately (since repression, e.g. administrative repression, may take non-physical forms).

I shall call Ideological State Apparatuses a certain number of realities which present themselves to the immediate observer in the form of distinct and specialized institutions. I propose an empirical list of these which will obviously have to be examined in detail, tested, corrected and re-organized. With all the reservations implied by this requirement, we can for the moment regard the following institutions as Ideological State Apparatuses (the order in which I have listed them has no particular significance):

– the religious ISA (the system of the different Churches),
– the educational ISA (the system of the different public and private 'Schools'),
– the family ISA,[8]
– the legal ISA,[9]
– the political ISA (the political system, including the different Parties),
– the trade-union ISA,
– the communications ISA (press, radio and television, etc.),
– the cultural ISA (Literature, the Arts, sports, etc.).

I have said that the ISAs must not be confused with the (Repressive) State Apparatus. What constitutes the difference?

8. The family obviously has other 'functions' than that of an ISA. It intervenes in the reproduction of labour power. In different modes of production it is the unit of production and/or the unit of consumption.
9. The 'Law' belongs both to the (Repressive) State Apparatus and to the system of the ISAs.

As a first moment, it is clear that while there is *one* (Repressive) State Apparatus, there is a *plurality* of Ideological State Apparatuses. Even presupposing that it exists, the unity that constitutes this plurality of ISAs as a body is not immediately visible.

As a second moment, it is clear that whereas the – unified – (Repressive) State Apparatus belongs entirely to the *public* domain, much the larger part of the Ideological State Apparatuses (in their apparent dispersion) are part, on the contrary, of the *private* domain. Churches, Parties, Trade Unions, families, some schools, most newspapers, cultural ventures, etc., etc., are private.

We can ignore the first observation for the moment. But someone is bound to question the second, asking me by what right I regard as Ideological *State* Apparatuses, institutions which for the most part do not possess public status, but are quite simply *private* institutions. As a conscious Marxist, Gramsci already forestalled this objection in one sentence. The distinction between the public and the private is a distinction internal to bourgeois law, and valid in the (subordinate) domains in which bourgeois law exercises its 'authority'. The domain of the State escapes it because the latter is 'above the law': the State, which is the State *of* the ruling class, is neither public nor private; on the contrary, it is the precondition for any distinction between public and private. The same thing can be said from the starting-point of our State Ideological Apparatuses. It is unimportant whether the institutions in which they are realized are 'public' or 'private'. What matters is how they function. Private institutions can perfectly well 'function' as Ideological State Apparatuses. A reasonably thorough analysis of any one of the ISAs proves it.

But now for what is essential. What distinguishes the ISAs from the (Repressive) State Apparatus is the following basic difference: the Repressive State Apparatus functions 'by violence', whereas the Ideological State Apparatuses *function 'by ideology'*.

I can clarify matters by correcting this distinction. I shall say rather that every State Apparatus, whether Repressive or Ideological, 'functions' both by violence and by ideology, but with one very important distinction which makes it imperative not to confuse the Ideological State Apparatuses with the (Repressive) State Apparatus.

This is the fact that the (Repressive) State Apparatus functions massively and predominantly *by repression* (including physical repression), while functioning secondarily by ideology. (There is no such thing as a purely repressive apparatus.) For example, the Army and the Police also function by ideology both to ensure their own cohesion and reproduction, and in the 'values' they propound externally.

In the same way, but inversely, it is essential to say that for their part the Ideological State Apparatuses function massively and predominantly *by ideology*, but they also function secondarily by repression, even if ultimately, but only ultimately, this is very attenuated and concealed, even symbolic. (There is no such thing as a purely ideological apparatus.) Thus Schools and Churches use suitable methods of punishment, expulsion, selection, etc., to 'discipline' not only their shepherds, but also their flocks. The same is true of the Family. . . . The same is true of the cultural IS Apparatus (censorship, among other things), etc.

Is it necessary to add that this determination of the double 'functioning' (predominantly, secondarily) by repression and by ideology, according to whether it is a matter of the (Repressive) State Apparatus or the Ideological State Apparatuses, makes it clear that very subtle explicit or tacit combinations may be woven from the interplay of the (Repressive) State Apparatus and the Ideological State Apparatuses? Everyday life provides us with innumerable examples of this, but they must be studied in detail if we are to go further than this mere observation.

Nevertheless, this remark leads us towards an understanding of what constitutes the unity of the apparently disparate body of the ISAs. If the ISAs 'function' massively and predominantly by ideology, what unifies their diversity is precisely this functioning, insofar as the ideology by which they function is always in fact unified, despite ·its diversity and its contradictions, *beneath the ruling ideology*, which is the ideology of 'the ruling class'. Given the fact that the 'ruling class' in principle holds State power (openly or more often by means of alliances between classes or class fractions), and therefore has at its disposal the (Repressive) State Apparatus, we can accept the fact that this same ruling ideology is active in the Ideological State Apparatuses the ruling ideology which is active in the Ideological State Apparatuses, precisely in its contradictions. Of course, it is a quite different thing to act by laws and decrees in the (Repressive) State Apparatus and to 'act' through the intermediary of the ruling ideology in the Ideological State Apparatuses. We must go into the details of this difference – but it cannot mask the reality of a profound identity. To my knowledge, *no class can hold State power over a long period without at the same time exercising its hegemony over and in the State Ideological Apparatuses.* I only need one example and proof of this: Lenin's anguished concern to revolutionize the educational Ideological State Apparatus (among others), simply to make it possible for the Soviet proletariat, who had seized State power, to secure the future of the dictatorship of the proletariat and the transition to socialism.[10]

10. In a pathetic text written in 1937, Krupskaya relates the history of Lenin's desperate efforts and what she regards as his failure.

This last comment puts us in a position to understand that the Ideological State Apparatuses may be not only the *stake*, but also the *site* of class struggle, and often of bitter forms of class struggle. The class (or class alliance) in power cannot lay down the law in the ISAs as easily as it can in the (repressive) State apparatus, not only because the former ruling classes are able to retain strong positions there for a long time, but also because the resistance of the exploited classes is able to find means and occasions to express itself there, either by the utilization of their contradictions, or by conquering combat positions in them in struggle.[11]

Let me run through my comments.

If the thesis I have proposed is well-founded, it leads me back to the classical Marxist theory of the State, while making it more precise in one point. I argue that it is necessary to distinguish between State power (and its possession by . . .) on the one hand, and the State Apparatus on the other. But I add that the State Apparatus contains

---

11. What I have said in these few brief words about the class struggle in the ISAs is obviously far from exhausting the question of the class struggle.

To approach this question, two principles must be borne in mind:

The first principle was formulated by Marx in the Preface to *A Contribution to the Critique of Political Economy*: 'In considering such transformations [a social revolution] a distinction should always be made between the material transformation of the economic conditions of production, which can be determined with the precision of natural science, and the legal, political, religious, aesthetic or philosophic – in short, ideological forms in which men become conscious of this conflict and fight it out.' The class struggle is thus expressed and exercised in ideological forms, thus also in the ideological forms of the ISAs. But the class struggle *extends far beyond* these forms, and it is because it extends beyond them that the struggle of the exploited classes may also be exercised in the forms of the ISAs, and thus turn the weapon of ideology against the classes in power.

This by virtue of the *second principle*: the class struggle extends beyond the ISAs because it is rooted elsewhere than in ideology, in the Infrastructure, in the relations of production, which are relations of exploitation and constitute the base for class relations.

two bodies: the body of institutions which represent the Repressive State Apparatus on the one hand, and the body of institutions which represent the body of Ideological State Apparatuses on the other.

But if this is the case, the following question is bound to be asked, even in the very summary state of my suggestions: what exactly is the extent of the role of the Ideological State Apparatuses? What is their importance based on? In other words: to what does the 'function' of these Ideological State Apparatuses, which do not function by repression but by ideology, correspond?

ON THE REPRODUCTION OF THE RELATIONS OF PRODUCTION

I can now answer the central question which I have left in suspense for many long pages: *how is the reproduction of the relations of production secured?*

In the topographical language (Infrastructure, Super-structure), I can say: for the most part,[12] it is secured by the legal-political and ideological superstructure.

But as I have argued that it is essential to go beyond this still descriptive language, I shall say: for the most part,[12] it is secured by the exercise of State power in the State Apparatuses, on the one hand the (Repressive) State Apparatus, on the other the Ideological State Apparatuses.

What I have just said must also be taken into account, and it can be assembled in the form of the following three features:

12. For the most part. For the relations of production are first reproduced by the materiality of the processes of production and circulation. But it should not be forgotten that ideological relations are immediately present in these same processes.

1. All the State Apparatuses function both by repression and by ideology, with the difference that the (Repressive) State Apparatus functions massively and predominantly by repression, whereas the Ideological State Apparatuses function massively and predominantly by ideology.

2. Whereas the (Repressive) State Apparatus constitutes an organized whole whose different parts are centralized beneath a commanding unity, that of the politics of class struggle applied by the political representatives of the ruling classes in possession of State power, the Ideological State Apparatuses are multiple, distinct, 'relatively autonomous' and capable of providing an objective field to contradictions which express, in forms which may be limited or extreme, the effects of the clashes between the capitalist class struggle and the proletarian class struggle, as well as their subordinate forms.

3. Whereas the unity of the (Repressive) State Apparatus is secured by its unified and centralized organization under the leadership of the representatives of the classes in power executing the politics of the class struggle of the classes in power, the unity of the different Ideological State Apparatuses is secured, usually in contradictory forms, by the ruling ideology, the ideology of the ruling class.

Taking these features into account, it is possible to represent the reproduction of the relations of production[13] in the following way, according to a kind of 'division of labour'.

The role of the repressive State apparatus, insofar as it is a repressive apparatus, consists essentially in securing by force (physical or otherwise) the political conditions of the reproduction of relations of production which are in the

13. *For that part* of reproduction to which the Repressive State Apparatus and the Ideological State Apparatus *contribute*.

last resort *relations of exploitation*. Not only does the State apparatus contribute generously to its own reproduction (the capitalist State contains political dynasties, military dynasties, etc.), but also and above all, the State apparatus secures by repression (from the most brutal physical force, via mere administrative commands and interdictions, to open and tacit censorship) the political conditions for the action of the Ideological State Apparatuses.

In fact, it is the latter which largely secure the reproduction specifically of the relations of production, behind a 'shield' provided by the repressive State apparatus. It is here that the role of the ruling ideology is heavily concentrated, the ideology of the ruling class, which holds State power. It is the intermediation of the ruling ideology that ensures a (sometimes teeth-gritting) 'harmony' between the repressive State apparatus and the Ideological State Apparatuses, and between the different State Ideological Apparatuses.

We are thus led to envisage the following hypothesis, as a function precisely of the diversity of ideological State Apparatuses in their single, because shared, role of the reproduction of the relations of production.

Indeed we have listed a relatively large number of ideological State apparatuses in contemporary capitalist social formations: the educational apparatus, the religious apparatus, the family apparatus, the political apparatus, the trade-union apparatus, the communications apparatus, the 'cultural' apparatus, etc.

But in the social formations of that mode of production characterized by 'serfdom' (usually called the feudal mode of production), we observe that although there is a single repressive State apparatus which, since the earliest known Ancient States, let alone the Absolute Monarchies, has been formally very similar to the one we know today, the number of Ideological State Apparatuses is smaller and their individual types are different. For example, we observe that during the Middle Ages, the Church (the religious ideological State apparatus) accumulated a number of functions which have today devolved on to several distinct ideological State apparatuses, new ones in relation to the past I am invoking, in particular educational and cultural functions. Alongside the Church there was the family Ideological State Apparatus, which played a considerable part, incommensurable with its role in capitalist social formations. Despite appearances, the Church and the Family were not the only Ideological State Apparatuses. There was also a political Ideological State Apparatus (the Estates General, the *Parlement*, the different political factions and Leagues, the ancestors or the modern political parties, and the whole political system of the free Communes and then of the *Villes*). There was also a powerful 'proto-trade-union' Ideological State Apparatus, if I may venture such an anachronistic term (the powerful merchants' and bankers' guilds and the journeymen's associations, etc.). Publishing and Communications, even, saw an indisputable development, as did the theatre; initially both were integral parts of the Church, then they became more and more independent of it.

In the pre-capitalist historical period which I have examined extremely broadly, it is absolutely clear that *there was one dominant Ideological State Apparatus, the Church*, which concentrated within it not only religious functions, but also educational ones, and a large proportion of the functions of communications and 'culture'. It is no accident that all ideological struggle, from the sixteenth to the eighteenth century, starting with the first shocks of the Reformation, was *concentrated* in an anti-clerical and anti-religious struggle; rather this is a function precisely of the dominant position of the religious ideological State apparatus.

The foremost objective and achievement of the French

Revolution was not just to transfer State power from the feudal aristocracy to the merchant-capitalist bourgeoisie, to break part of the former repressive State apparatus and replace it with a new one (e.g., the national popular Army) – but also to attack the number-one Ideological State Apparatus: the Church. Hence the civil constitution of the clergy, the confiscation of ecclesiastical wealth, and the creation of new ideological State apparatuses to replace the religious ideological State apparatus in its dominant role.

Naturally, these things did not happen automatically: witness the Concordat, the Restoration and the long class struggle between the landed aristocracy and the industrial bourgeoisie throughout the nineteenth century for the establishment of bourgeois hegemony over the functions formerly fulfilled by the Church: above all by the Schools. It can be said that the bourgeoisie relied on the new political, parliamentary-democratic, ideological State apparatus, installed in the earliest years of the Revolution, then restored after long and violent struggles, for a few months in 1848 and for decades after the fall of the Second Empire, in order to conduct its struggle against the Church and wrest its ideological functions away from it, in other words, to ensure not only its own political hegemony, but also the ideological hegemony indispensable to the reproduction of capitalist relations of production.

That is why I believe that I am justified in advancing the following Thesis, however precarious it is. I believe that the ideological State apparatus which has been installed in the *dominant* position in mature capitalist social formations as a result of a violent political and ideological class struggle against the old dominant ideological State apparatus, is the *educational ideological apparatus.*

This thesis may seem paradoxical, given that for everyone, i.e. in the ideological representation that the bourgeoisie has tried to give itself and the classes it exploits, it really seems that the dominant ideological State apparatus in capitalist social formations is not the Schools, but the political ideological State apparatus, i.e. the regime of parliamentary democracy combining universal suffrage and party struggle.

However, history, even recent history, shows that the bourgeoisie has been and still is able to accommodate itself to political ideological State apparatuses other than parliamentary democracy: the First and Second Empires, Constitutional Monarchy (Louis XVIII and Charles X), Parliamentary Monarchy (Louis-Philippe), Presidential Democracy (de Gaulle), to mention only France. In England this is even clearer. The Revolution was particularly 'successful' there from the bourgeois point of view, since unlike France, where the bourgeoisie, partly because of the stupidity of the petty aristocracy, had to agree to being carried to power by peasant and plebeian *'journées révolutionnaires'*, something for which it had to pay a high price, the English bourgeoisie was able to 'compromise' with the aristocracy and 'share' State power and the use of the State apparatus with it for a long time (peace among all men of good will in the ruling classes!). In Germany it is even more striking, since it was behind a political ideological State apparatus in which the imperial Junkers (epitomized by Bismarck), their army and their police provided it with a shield and leading personnel, that the imperialist bourgeoisie made its shattering entry into history, before 'traversing' the Weimar Republic and entrusting itself to Nazism.

Hence I believe I have good reasons for thinking that behind the scenes of its political Ideological State Apparatus, which occupies the front of the stage, what the bourgeoisie has installed as its number-one, i.e. as its dominant ideological State apparatus, is the educational apparatus, which has in fact replaced in its functions the previously dominant ideological State apparatus, the Church. One might even add: the School-Family couple has replaced the Church-Family couple.

Why is the educational apparatus in fact the dominant ideological State apparatus in capitalist social formations, and how does it function?

For the moment it must suffice to say:

1. All ideological State apparatuses, whatever they are, contribute to the same result: the reproduction of the relations of production, i.e. of capitalist relations of exploitation.

2. Each of them contributes towards this single result in the way proper to it. The political apparatus by subjecting individuals to the political State ideology, the 'indirect' (parliamentary) or 'direct' (plebiscitary or fascist) 'democratic' ideology. The communications apparatus by cramming every 'citizen' with daily doses of nationalism, chauvinism, liberalism, moralism, etc, by means of the press, the radio and television. The same goes for the cultural apparatus (the role of sport in chauvinism is of the first importance), etc. The religious apparatus by recalling in sermons and the other great ceremonies of Birth, Marriage and Death, that man is only ashes, unless he loves his neighbour to the extent of turning the other cheek to whoever strikes first. The family apparatus . . . but there is no need to go on.

3. This concert is dominated by a single score, occasionally disturbed by contradictions (those of the remnants of former ruling classes, those of the proletarians and their organizations): the score of the Ideology of the current ruling class which integrates into its music the great themes of the Humanism of the Great Forefathers, who produced the Greek Miracle even before Christianity, and afterwards

so totalizing & depressing

the Glory of Rome, the Eternal City, and the themes of Interest, particular and general, etc. nationalism, moralism and economism.

4. Nevertheless, in this concert, one ideological State apparatus certainly has the dominant role, although hardly anyone lends an ear to its music: it is so silent! This is the School.

It takes children from every class at infant-school age, and then for years, the years in which the child is most 'vulnerable', squeezed between the family State apparatus and the educational State apparatus, it drums into them, whether it uses new or old methods, a certain amount of 'know-how' wrapped in the ruling ideology (French, arithmetic, natural history, the sciences, literature) or simply the ruling ideology in its pure state (ethics, civic instruction, philosophy). Somewhere around the age of sixteen, a huge mass of children are ejected 'into production': these are the workers or small peasants. Another portion of scholastically adapted youth carries on: and, for better or worse, it goes somewhat further, until it falls by the wayside and fills the posts of small and middle technicians, white-collar workers, small and middle executives, petty bourgeois of all kinds. A last portion reaches the summit, either to fall into intellectual semi-employment, or to provide, as well as the 'intellectuals of the collective labourer', the agents of exploitation (capitalists, managers), the agents of repression (soldiers, policemen, politicians, administrators, etc.) and the professional ideologists (priests of all sorts, most of whom are convinced 'laymen').

Each mass ejected *en route* is practically provided with the ideology which suits the role it has to fulfil in class society: the role of the exploited (with a 'highly-developed' 'professional', 'ethical', 'civic', 'national' and a-political consciousness); the role of the agent of exploitation (ability to give the workers orders and speak to them: 'human relations'), of the agent of repression (ability to give orders and enforce obedience 'without discussion', or ability to manipulate the demagogy of a political leader's rhetoric), or of the professional ideologist (ability to treat conscious-nesses with the respect, i.e. with the contempt, blackmail, and demagogy they deserve, adapted to the accents of Morality, of Virtue, of 'Transcendence', of the Nation, of France's World Role, etc.).

Of course, many of these contrasting Virtues (modesty, resignation, submissiveness on the one hand, cynicism, contempt, arrogance, confidence, self-importance, even smooth talk and cunning on the other) are also taught in the Family, in the Church, in the Army, in Good Books, in films and even in the football stadium. But no other ideo-logical State apparatus has the obligatory (and not least, free) audience of the totality of the children in the capitalist social formation, eight hours a day for five or six days out of seven.

But it is by an apprenticeship in a variety of know-how wrapped up in the massive inculcation of the ideology of the ruling class that the *relations of production* in a capitalist social formation, i.e. the relations of exploited to exploiters and exploiters to exploited, are largely reproduced. The mechanisms which produce this vital result for the capitalist regime are naturally covered up and concealed by a univer-sally reigning ideology of the School, universally reigning because it is one of the essential forms of the ruling bour-geois ideology: an ideology which represents the School as a neutral environment purged of ideology (because it is . . . lay), where teachers respectful of the 'conscience' and 'freedom' of the children who are entrusted to them (in complete confidence) by their 'parents' (who are free, too, i.e. the owners of their children) open up for them the path to the freedom, morality and responsibility of adults by their own example, by knowledge, literature and their 'liberating' virtues.

I ask the pardon of those teachers who, in dreadful conditions, attempt to turn the few weapons they can find in the history and learning they 'teach' against the ideology, the system and the practices in which they are trapped. They are a kind of hero. But they are rare and how many (the majority) do not even begin to suspect the 'work' the system (which is bigger than they are and crushes them) forces them to do, or worse, put all their heart and ingenuity into performing it with the most advanced awareness (the famous new methods!). So little do they suspect it that their own devotion contributes to the maintenance and nourishment of this ideological representation of the School, which makes the School today as 'natural', indispensable-useful and even beneficial for our contemporaries as the Church was 'natural', indispensable and generous for our ancestors a few centuries ago.

In fact, the Church has been replaced today *in its role as the dominant Ideological State Apparatus* by the School. It is coupled with the Family just as the Church was once coupled with the Family. We can now claim that the unprecedentedly deep crisis which is now shaking the education system of so many States across the globe, often in conjunction with a crisis (already proclaimed in the *Communist Manifesto*) shaking the family system, takes on a political meaning, given that the School (and the School-Family couple) constitutes the dominant Ideological State Apparatus, the Apparatus playing a determinant part in the reproduction of the relations of production of a mode of production threatened in its existence by the world class struggle.

ON IDEOLOGY

When I put forward the concept of an Ideological State Apparatus, when I said that the ISAs 'function by ideology', I invoked a reality which needs a little discussion: ideology.

It is well known that the expression 'ideology' was invented by Cabanis, Destutt de Tracy and their friends, who assigned to it as an object the (genetic) theory of ideas. When Marx took up the term fifty years later, he gave it a quite different meaning, even in his Early Works. Here, ideology is the system of the ideas and representations which dominate the mind of a man or a social group. The ideologico-political struggle conducted by Marx as early as his articles in the *Rheinische Zeitung* inevitably and quickly brought him face to face with this reality and forced him to take his earliest intuitions further.

However, here we come upon a rather astonishing paradox. Everything seems to lead Marx to formulate a theory of ideology. In fact, *The German Ideology* does offer us, after the *1844 Manuscripts*, an explicit theory of ideology, but . . . it is not Marxist (we shall see why in a moment). As for *Capital*, although it does contain many hints towards a theory of ideologies (most visibly, the ideology of the vulgar economists), it does not contain that theory itself, which depends for the most part on a theory of ideology in general.

I should like to venture a first and very schematic outline of such a theory. The theses I am about to put forward are certainly not off the cuff, but they cannot be sustained and tested, i.e. confirmed or rejected, except by much thorough study and analysis.

Ideology has no History

One word first of all to expound the reason in principle which seems to me to found, or at least to justify, the project of a theory of ideology *in general*, and not a theory of particular ideolog*ies*, which, whatever their form (religious, ethical, legal, political), always express *class positions*.

It is quite obvious that it is necessary to proceed towards a theory of ideolog*ies* in the two respects I have just suggested. It will then be clear that a theory of ideolog*ies* depends in the last resort on the history of social formations, and thus of the modes of production combined in social formations, and of the class struggles which develop in them. In this sense it is clear that there can be no question of a theory of ideolog*ies in general*, since ideolog*ies* (defined in the double respect suggested above: regional and class) have a history, whose determination in the last instance is clearly situated outside ideologies alone, although it involves them.

On the contrary, if I am able to put forward the project of a theory of ideology *in general*, and if this theory really is one of the elements on which theories of ideolog*ies* depend, that entails an apparently paradoxical proposition which I shall express in the following terms: *ideology has no history*.

As we know, this formulation appears in so many words in a passage from *The German Ideology*. Marx utters it with respect to metaphysics, which, he says, has no more history than ethics (meaning also the other forms of ideology).

In *The German Ideology*, this formulation appears in a plainly positivist context. Ideology is conceived as a pure illusion, a pure dream, i.e. as nothingness. All its reality is external to it. Ideology is thus thought as an imaginary construction whose status is exactly like the theoretical status of the dream among writers before Freud. For these writers, the dream was the purely imaginary, i.e. null,

result of 'day's residues', presented in an arbitrary arrange-
ment and order, sometimes even 'inverted', in other words,
in 'disorder'. For them, the dream was the imaginary, it
was empty, null and arbitrarily 'stuck together' (*bricolé*),
once the eyes had closed, from the residues of the only full
and positive reality, the reality of the day. This is exactly
the status of philosophy and ideology (since in this book
philosophy is ideology *par excellence*) in *The German Ideology*.

Ideology, then, is for Marx an imaginary assemblage
(*bricolage*), a pure dream, empty and vain, constituted by
the 'day's residues' from the only full and positive reality,
that of the concrete history of concrete material individuals
materially producing their existence. It is on this basis that
ideology has no history in *The German Ideology*, since its
history is outside it, where the only existing history is,
the history of concrete individuals, etc. In *The German
Ideology*, the thesis that ideology has no history is therefore
a purely negative thesis, since it means both:

1. ideology is nothing insofar as it is a pure dream (manu-
factured by who knows what power: if not by the alienation
of the division of labour, but that, too, is a *negative* determination);

2. ideology has no history, which emphatically does not
mean that there is no history in it (on the contrary, for it is
merely the pale, empty and inverted reflection of real
history) but that it has no history *of its own*.

Now, while the thesis I wish to defend formally speaking
adopts the terms of *The German Ideology* ('ideology has no
history'), it is radically different from the positivist and
historicist thesis of *The German Ideology*.

For on the one hand, I think it is possible to hold that
ideolog*ies have a history of their own* (although it is determined in the last instance by the class struggle); and on the
other, I think it is possible to hold that ideology *in general*

has no history, not in a negative sense (its history is external to it), but in an absolutely positive sense.

This sense is a positive one if it is true that the peculiarity of ideology is that it is endowed with a structure and a functioning such as to make it a non-historical reality, i.e. an *omni-historical* reality, in the sense in which that structure and functioning are immutable, present in the same form throughout what we can call history, in the sense in which the *Communist Manifesto* defines history as the history of class struggles, i.e. the history of class societies.

To give a theoretical reference-point here, I might say that, to return to our example of the dream, in its Freudian conception this time, our proposition: ideology has no history, can and must (and in a way which has absolutely nothing arbitrary about it, but, quite the reverse, is theoretically necessary, for there is an organic link between the two propositions) be related directly to Freud's proposition that the *unconscious is eternal*, i.e. that it has no history.

If eternal means, not transcendent to all (temporal) history, but omnipresent, trans-historical and therefore immutable in form throughout the extent of history, I shall adopt Freud's expression word for word, and write *ideology is eternal*, exactly like the unconscious. And I add that I find this comparison theoretically justified by the fact that the eternity of the unconscious is not unrelated to the eternity of ideology in general.

That is why I believe I am justified, hypothetically at least, in proposing a theory of ideology *in general*, in the sense that Freud presented a theory of the unconscious *in general*.

To simplify the phrase, it is convenient, taking into account what has been said about ideologies, to use the plain term ideology to designate ideology in general, which I have just said has no history, or, what comes to the same thing, is eternal, i.e. omnipresent in its immutable form throughout history (= the history of social formations containing social classes). For the moment I shall restrict myself to 'class societies' and their history.

Ideology is a 'Representation' of the Imaginary Relationship of Individuals to their Real Conditions of Existence

In order to approach my central thesis on the structure and functioning of ideology, I shall first present two theses, one negative, the other positive. The first concerns the object which is 'represented' in the imaginary form of ideology, the second concerns the materiality of ideology.

THESIS I: <u>Ideology represents the imaginary relation-ship of individuals to their real conditions of existence.</u>

We commonly call religious ideology, ethical ideology, legal ideology, political ideology, etc., so many 'world outlooks'. Of course, assuming that we do not live one of these ideologies as the truth (e.g. 'believe' in God, Duty, Justice, etc. . . .), we admit that the ideology we are discussing from a critical point of view, examining it as the ethnologist examines the myths of a 'primitive society', that these 'world outlooks' are largely imaginary, i.e. do not 'correspond to reality'.

However, while admitting that they do not correspond to reality, i.e. that they constitute an illusion, we admit that they do make allusion to reality, and that they need only be 'interpreted' to discover the reality of the world behind their imaginary representation of that world (ideology = *illusion/allusion*).

There are different types of interpretation, the most famous of which are the *mechanistic* type, current in the eighteenth century (God is the imaginary representation of the real King), and the *'hermeneutic'* interpretation, inaugurated by the earliest Church Fathers, and revived by

Feuerbach and the theologico-philosophical school which descends from him, e.g. the theologian Barth (to Feuerbach, for example, God is the essence of real Man). The essential point is that on condition that we interpret the imaginary transposition (and inversion) of ideology we arrive at the conclusion that in ideology 'men represent their real conditions of existence to themselves in an imaginary form'.

Unfortunately, this interpretation leaves one small problem unsettled: why do men 'need' this imaginary transposition of their real conditions of existence in order to 'represent to themselves' their real conditions of existence?

The first answer (that of the eighteenth century) proposes a simple solution: Priests or Despots are responsible. They 'forged' the Beautiful Lies so that, in the belief that they were obeying God, men would in fact obey the Priests and Despots, who are usually in alliance in their imposture, the Priests acting in the interests of the Despots or *vice versa*, according to the political positions of the 'theoreticians' concerned. There is therefore a cause for the imaginary transposition of the real conditions of existence: that cause is the existence of a small number of cynical men who base their domination and exploitation of the 'people' on a falsified representation of the world which they have imagined in order to enslave other minds by dominating their imaginations.

The second answer (that of Feuerbach, taken over word for word by Marx in his Early Works) is more 'profound', i.e. just as false. It, too, seeks and finds a cause for the imaginary transposition and distortion of men's real conditions of existence, in short, for the alienation in the imaginary of the representation of men's conditions of existence. This cause is no longer Priests or Despots, nor their active imagination and the passive imagination of their victims. This cause is the material alienation which reigns in the conditions of existence of men themselves. This is how, in *The Jewish Question* and elsewhere, Marx defends the Feuerbachian idea that men make themselves an alienated (= imaginary) representation of their conditions of existence because these conditions of existence are themselves alienating (in the *1844 Manuscripts*: because these conditions are dominated by the essence of alienated society – '*alienated labour*').

All these interpretations thus take literally the thesis which they presuppose, and on which they depend, i.e. that what is reflected in the imaginary representation of the world found in an ideology is the conditions of existence of men, i.e. their real world.

Now I can return to a thesis which I have already advanced: it is not their real conditions of existence, their real world, that 'men' 'represent to themselves' in ideology, but above all it is their relation to those conditions of existence which is represented to them there. It is this relation which is at the centre of every ideological, i.e. imaginary, representation of the real world. It is this relation that contains the 'cause' which has to explain the imaginary distortion of the ideological representation of the real world. Or rather, to leave aside the language of causality it is necessary to advance the thesis that it is the *imaginary nature of this relation* which underlies all the imaginary distortion that we can observe (if we do not live in its truth) in all ideology.

To speak in a Marxist language, if it is true that the representation of the real conditions of existence of the individuals occupying the posts of agents of production, exploitation, repression, ideologization and scientific practice, does in the last analysis arise from the relations of production, and from relations deriving from the relations of production, we can say the following: all ideology represents in its necessarily imaginary distortion not the existing relations of production (and the other relations that derive from them), but above all the (imaginary) relationship of individuals to the relations of production and the relations that derive from them. What is represented in ideology is therefore not the system of the real relations which govern the existence of individuals, but the imaginary relation of those individuals to the real relations in which they live.

If this is the case, the question of the 'cause' of the imaginary distortion of the real relations in ideology disappears and must be replaced by a different question: why is the representation given to individuals of their (individual) relation to the social relations which govern their conditions of existence and their collective and individual life necessarily an imaginary relation? And what is the nature of this imaginariness? Posed in this way, the question explodes the solution by a 'clique'[14], by a group of individuals (Priests or Despots) who are the authors of the great ideological mystification, just as it explodes the solution by the alienated character of the real world. We shall see why later in my exposition. For the moment I shall go no further.

THESIS II: Ideology has a material existence.

I have already touched on this thesis by saying that the 'ideas' or 'representations', etc., which seem to make up ideology do not have an ideal (*idéale* or *idéelle*) or spiritual existence, but a material existence. I even suggested that the ideal (*idéale*, *idéelle*) and spiritual existence of 'ideas' arises exclusively in an ideology of the 'idea' and of ideology, and let me add, in an ideology of what seems to have 'founded' this conception since the emergence of the sciences, i.e. what

14. I use this very modern term deliberately. For even in Communist circles, unfortunately, it is a commonplace to 'explain' some political deviation (left or right opportunism) by the action of a 'clique'.

the practicians of the sciences represent to themselves in their spontaneous ideology as 'ideas', true or false. Of course, presented in affirmative form, this thesis is unproven. I simply ask that the reader be favourably disposed towards it, say, in the name of materialism. A long series of arguments would be necessary to prove it.

This hypothetical thesis of the not spiritual but material existence of 'ideas' or other 'representations' is indeed necessary if we are to advance in our analysis of the nature of ideology. Or rather, it is merely useful to us in order the better to reveal what every at all serious analysis of any ideology will immediately and empirically show to every observer, however critical.

While discussing the ideological State apparatuses and their practices, I said that each of them was the realization of an ideology (the unity of these different regional ideologies – religious, ethical, legal, political, aesthetic, etc. being assured by their subjection to the ruling ideology). I now return to this thesis: an ideology always exists in an apparatus, and its practice, or practices. This existence is material.

Of course, the material existence of the ideology in an apparatus and its practices does not have the same modality as the material existence of a paving-stone or a rifle. But, at the risk of being taken for a Neo-Aristotelian (NB Marx had a very high regard for Aristotle), I shall say that 'matter is discussed in many senses', or rather that it exists in different modalities, all rooted in the last instance in 'physical' matter.

Having said this, let me move straight on and see what happens to the 'individuals' who live in ideology, i.e. in a determinate (religious, ethical, etc.) representation of the world whose imaginary distortion depends on their imaginary relation to their conditions of existence, in other words, in the last instance, to the relations of production

interesting formulation: living in ideology

and to class relations (ideology = an imaginary relation to real relations). I shall say that this imaginary relation is itself endowed with a material existence.

Now I observe the following.

An individual believes in God, or Duty, or Justice, etc. This belief derives (for everyone, i.e. for all those who live in an ideological representation of ideology, which reduces ideology to ideas endowed by definition with a spiritual existence) from the ideas of the individual concerned, i.e. from him as a subject with a consciousness which contains the ideas of his belief. In this way, i.e. by means of the absolutely ideological 'conceptual' device (*dispositif*) thus set up (a subject endowed with a consciousness in which he freely forms or freely recognizes ideas in which he believes), the (material) attitude of the subject concerned naturally follows.

The individual in question behaves in such and such a way, adopts such and such a practical attitude, and, what is more, participates in certain regular practices which are those of the ideological apparatus on which 'depend' the ideas which he has in all consciousness freely chosen as a subject. If he believes in God, he goes to Church to attend Mass, kneels, prays, confesses, does penance (once it was material in the ordinary sense of the term) and naturally repents and so on. If he believes in Duty, he will have the corresponding attitudes, inscribed in ritual practices 'according to the correct principles'. If he believes in Justice, he will submit unconditionally to the rules of the Law, and may even protest when they are violated, sign petitions, take part in a demonstration, etc.

Throughout this schema we observe that the ideological representation of ideology is itself forced to recognize that every 'subject' endowed with a 'consciousness' and believing in the 'ideas' that his 'consciousness' inspires in him and freely accepts, must '*act* according to his ideas', must therefore inscribe his own ideas as a free subject in the actions of his material practice. If he does not do so, 'that is wicked'.

Indeed, if he does not do what he ought to do as a function of what he believes, it is because he does something else, which, still as a function of the same idealist scheme, implies that he has other ideas in his head as well as those he proclaims, and that he acts according to these other ideas, as a man who is either 'inconsistent' ('no one is willingly evil') or cynical, or perverse.

In every case, the ideology of ideology thus recognizes, despite its imaginary distortion, that the 'ideas' of a human subject exist in his actions, or ought to exist in his actions, and if that is not the case, it lends him other ideas corresponding to the actions (however perverse) that he does perform. This ideology talks of actions: I shall talk of actions inserted into *practices*. *And* I shall point out that these practices are governed by the *rituals* in which these practices are inscribed, within the *material existence of an ideological apparatus*, be it only a small part of that apparatus: a small mass in a small church, a funeral, a minor match at a sports' club, a school day, a political party meeting, etc.

Besides, we are indebted to Pascal's defensive 'dialectic' for the wonderful formula which will enable us to invert the order of the notional schema of ideology. Pascal says more or less: 'Kneel down, move your lips in prayer, and you will believe.' He thus scandalously inverts the order of things, bringing, like Christ, not peace but strife, and in addition something hardly Christian (for woe to him who brings scandal into the world!) – scandal itself. A fortunate scandal which makes him stick with Jansenist defiance to a language that directly names the reality.

I will be allowed to leave Pascal to the arguments of his

ideological struggle with the religious ideological State apparatus of his day. And I shall be expected to use a more directly Marxist vocabulary, if that is possible, for we are advancing in still poorly explored domains.

I shall therefore say that, where only a single subject (such and such an individual) is concerned, the existence of the ideas of his belief is material in that *his ideas are his material actions inserted into material practices governed by material rituals which are themselves defined by the material ideological apparatus from which derive the ideas of that subject*. Naturally, the four inscriptions of the adjective 'material' in my proposition must be affected by different modalities: the materialities of a displacement for going to mass, of kneeling down, of the gesture of the sign of the cross, or of the *mea culpa*, of a sentence, of a prayer, of an act of contrition, of a penitence, of a gaze, of a hand-shake, of an external verbal discourse or an 'internal' verbal discourse (consciousness), are not one and the same materiality. I shall leave on one side the problem of a theory of the differences between the modalities of materiality.

It remains that in this inverted presentation of things, we are not dealing with an 'inversion' at all, since it is clear that certain notions have purely and simply disappeared from our presentation, whereas others on the contrary survive, and new terms appear.

Disappeared: the term *ideas*.

Survive: the terms *subject, consciousness, belief, actions*.

Appear: the terms *practices, rituals, ideological apparatus*.

It is therefore not an inversion or overturning (except in the sense in which one might say a government or a glass is overturned), but a reshuffle (of a non-ministerial type), a rather strange reshuffle, since we obtain the following result.

Ideas have disappeared as such (insofar as they are endowed with an ideal or spiritual existence), to the precise extent that it has emerged that their existence is inscribed in the actions of practices governed by rituals defined in the last instance by an ideological apparatus. It therefore appears that the subject acts insofar as he is acted by the following system (set out in the order of its real determination): ideology existing in a material ideological apparatus, prescribing material practices governed by a material ritual, which practices exist in the material actions of a subject acting in all consciousness according to his belief.

But this very presentation reveals that we have retained the following notions: subject, consciousness, belief, actions. From this series I shall immediately extract the decisive central term on which everything else depends: the notion of the *subject*.

And I shall immediately set down two conjoint theses:

1. there is no practice except by and in an ideology;

2. there is no ideology except by the subject and for subjects.

I can now come to my central thesis.

Ideology Interpellates Individuals as Subjects

This thesis is simply a matter of making my last proposition explicit: there is no ideology except by the subject and for subjects. Meaning, there is no ideology except for concrete subjects, and this destination for ideology is only made possible by the subject: meaning, *by the category of the subject* and its functioning.

By this I mean that, even if it only appears under this name (the subject) with the rise of bourgeois ideology, above all with the rise of legal ideology,[15] the category of the

15. Which borrowed the legal category of 'subject in law' to make an ideological notion: man is by nature a subject.

[handwritten note: Saying that ideology constitutes subjects as such. How?]

s............................... r other names: e.g., as the
s............................... e constitutive category of
a............................... nation (regional or class)
a............................... – since ideology has no
history.

I say: the category of the subject is constitutive of all ideology, but at the same time and immediately I add that *the category of the subject is only constitutive of all ideology insofar as all ideology has the function (which defines it) of 'constituting' concrete individuals as subjects*. In the interaction of this double constitution exists the functioning of all ideology, ideology being nothing but its functioning in the material forms of existence of that functioning.

In order to grasp what follows, it is essential to realize that both he who is writing these lines and the reader who reads them are themselves subjects, and therefore ideological subjects (a tautological proposition), i.e. that the author and the reader of these lines both live 'spontaneously' or 'naturally' in ideology in the sense in which I have said that 'man is an ideological animal by nature'.

That the author, insofar as he writes the lines of a discourse which claims to be scientific, is completely absent as a 'subject' from 'his' scientific discourse (for all scientific discourse is by definition a subject-less discourse, there is no 'Subject of science' except in an ideology of science) is a different question which I shall leave on one side for the moment.

As St Paul admirably put it, it is in the 'Logos', meaning in ideology, that we 'live, move and have our being'. It follows that, for you and for me, the category of the subject is a primary 'obviousness' (obviousnesses are always primary): it is clear that you and I are subjects (free, ethical, etc. . . .). Like all obviousnesses, including those that make a word 'name a thing' or 'have a meaning' (therefore including the obviousness of the 'transparency' of language), the 'obviousness' that you and I are subjects – and that that does not cause any problems – is an ideological effect, the elementary ideological effect.[16] It is indeed a peculiarity of ideology that it imposes (without appearing to do so, since these are 'obviousnesses') obviousnesses as obviousnesses, which we cannot *fail to recognize* and before which we have the inevitable and natural reaction of crying out (aloud or in the 'still, small voice of conscience'): 'That's obvious! That's right! That's true!'

At work in this reaction is the ideological *recognition* function which is one of the two functions of ideology as such (its inverse being the function of *misrecognition* – *méconnaissance*).

To take a highly 'concrete' example, we all have friends who, when they knock on our door and we ask, through the door, the question 'Who's there?', answer (since 'it's obvious') 'It's me'. And we recognize that 'it is him', or 'her'. We open the door, and 'it's true, it really was she who was there'. To take another example, when we recognize somebody of our (previous) acquaintance ((*re*)-*connaissance*) in the street, we show him that we have recognized him (and have recognized that he has recognized us) by saying to him 'Hello, my friend', and shaking his hand (a material ritual practice of ideological recognition in everyday life – in France, at least; elsewhere, there are other rituals).

In this preliminary remark and these concrete illustrations, I only wish to point out that you and I are *always already* subjects, and as such constantly practice the rituals of ideological recognition, which guarantee for us that we

16. Linguists and those who appeal to linguistics for various purposes often run up against difficulties which arise because they ignore the action of the ideological effects in all discourses – including even scientific discourses.

are indeed concrete, individual, distinguishable and (naturally) irreplaceable subjects. The writing I am currently executing and the reading you are currently[17] performing are also in this respect rituals of ideological recognition, including the 'obviousness' with which the 'truth' or 'error' of my reflections may impose itself on you.

But to recognize that we are subjects and that we function in the practical rituals of the most elementary everyday life (the hand-shake, the fact of calling you by your name, the fact of knowing, even if I do not know what it is, that you 'have' a name of your own, which means that you are recognized as a unique subject, etc.) – this recognition only gives us the 'consciousness' of our incessant (eternal) practice of ideological recognition – its consciousness, i.e. its *recognition* – but in no sense does it give us the (scientific) *knowledge* of the mechanism of this recognition. Now it is this knowledge that we have to reach, if you will, while speaking in ideology, and from within ideology we have to outline a discourse which tries to break with ideology, in order to dare to be the beginning of a scientific (i.e. subjectless) discourse on ideology.

Thus in order to represent why the category of the 'subject' is constitutive of ideology, which only exists by constituting concrete subjects as subjects, I shall employ a special mode of exposition: 'concrete' enough to be recognized, but abstract enough to be thinkable and thought, giving rise to a knowledge.

As a first formulation I shall say: *all ideology hails or interpellates concrete individuals as concrete subjects, by the functioning of the category of the subject.*

17. NB: this double 'currently' is one more proof of the fact that ideology is 'eternal', since these two 'currentlys' are separated by an indefinite interval; I am writing these lines on 6 April 1969, you may read them at any subsequent time.

This is a proposition which entails that we distinguish for the moment between concrete individuals on the one hand and concrete subjects on the other, although at this level concrete subjects only exist insofar as they are supported by a concrete individual.

I shall then suggest that ideology 'acts' or 'functions' in such a way that it 'recruits' subjects among the individuals (it recruits them all), or 'transforms' the individuals into subjects (it transforms them all) by that very precise operation which I have called *interpellation* or hailing, and which can be imagined along the lines of the most commonplace everyday police (or other) hailing: 'Hey, you there!'[18]

Assuming that the theoretical scene I have imagined takes place in the street, the hailed individual will turn round. By this mere one-hundred-and-eighty-degree physical conversion, he becomes a *subject*. Why? Because he has recognized that the hail was 'really' addressed to him, and that 'it was *really him* who was hailed' (and not someone else). Experience shows that the practical telecommunication of hailings is such that they hardly ever miss their man: verbal call or whistle, the one hailed always recognizes that it is really him who is being hailed. And yet it is a strange phenomenon, and one which cannot be explained solely by 'guilt feelings', despite the large numbers who 'have something on their consciences'.

Naturally for the convenience and clarity of my little theoretical theatre I have had to present things in the form of a sequence, with a before and an after, and thus in the form of a temporal succession. There are individuals walking along. Somewhere (usually behind them) the hail rings out: 'Hey, you there!' One individual (nine times out

18. Hailing as an everyday practice subject to a precise ritual takes a quite 'special' form in the policeman's practice of 'hailing' which concerns the hailing of 'suspects'.

of ten it is the right one) turns round, believing/suspecting/ knowing that it is for him, i.e. recognizing that 'it really is he' who is meant by the hailing. But in reality these things happen without any succession. The existence of ideology and the hailing or interpellation of individuals as subjects are one and the same thing.

I might add: what thus seems to take place outside ideology (to be precise, in the street), in reality takes place in ideology. What really takes place in ideology seems therefore to take place outside it. That is why those who are in ideology believe themselves by definition outside ideology: one of the effects of ideology is the practical *denegation* of the ideological character of ideology by ideology: ideology never says, 'I am ideological'. It is necessary to be outside ideology, i.e. in scientific knowledge, to be able to say: I am in ideology (a quite exceptional case) or (the general case): I was in ideology. As is well known, the accusation of being in ideology only applies to others, never to oneself (unless one is really a Spinozist or a Marxist, which, in this matter, is to be exactly the same thing). Which amounts to saying that ideology *has no outside* (for itself), but at the same time *that it is nothing but outside* (for science and reality).

Spinoza explained this completely two centuries before Marx, who practised it but without explaining it in detail. But let us leave this point, although it is heavy with consequences, consequences which are not just theoretical, but also directly political, since, for example, the whole theory of criticism and self-criticism, the golden rule of the Marxist-Leninist practice of the class struggle, depends on it.

Thus ideology hails or interpellates individuals as subjects. As ideology is eternal, I must now suppress the temporal form in which I have presented the functioning of ideology, and say: ideology has always-already interpellated individuals as subjects, which amounts to making it clear

spatial

that individuals are always-already interpellated by ideology as subjects, which necessarily leads us to one last proposition: *individuals are always-already subjects*. Hence individuals are 'abstract' with respect to the subjects which they always-already are. This proposition might seem paradoxical.

That an individual is always-already a subject, even before he is born, is nevertheless the plain reality, accessible to everyone and not a paradox at all. Freud shows that individuals are always 'abstract' with respect to the subjects they always-already are, simply by noting the ideological ritual that surrounds the expectation of a 'birth', that 'happy event'. Everyone knows how much and in what way an unborn child is expected. Which amounts to saying, very prosaically, if we agree to drop the 'sentiments', i.e. the forms of family ideology (paternal/maternal/conjugal/fraternal) in which the unborn child is expected: it is certain in advance that it will bear its Father's Name, and will therefore have an identity and be irreplaceable. Before its birth, the child is therefore always-already a subject, appointed as a subject in and by the specific familial ideological configuration in which it is 'expected' once it has been conceived. I hardly need add that this familial ideological configuration is, in its uniqueness, highly structured, and that it is in this implacable and more or less 'pathological' (presupposing that any meaning can be assigned to that term) structure that the former subject-to-be will have to 'find' 'its' place, i.e. 'become' the sexual subject (boy or girl) which it already is in advance. It is clear that this ideological constraint and pre-appointment, and all the rituals of rearing and then education in the family, have some relationship with what Freud studied in the forms of the pre-genital and genital 'stages' of sexuality, i.e. in the 'grip' of what Freud registered by its effects as being the unconscious. But let us leave this point, too, on one side.

Let me go one step further. What I shall now turn my attention to is the way the 'actors' in this *mise en scène* of interpellation, and their respective roles, are reflected in the very structure of all ideology.

An Example: The Christian Religious Ideology

As the formal structure of all ideology is always the same, I shall restrict my analysis to a single example, one accessible to everyone, that of religious ideology, with the proviso that the same demonstration can be produced for ethical, legal, political, aesthetic ideology, etc.

Let us therefore consider the Christian religious ideology. I shall use a rhetorical figure and 'make it speak', i.e. collect into a fictional discourse what it 'says' not only in its two Testaments, its Theologians, Sermons, but also in its practices, its rituals, its ceremonies and its sacraments. The Christian religious ideology says something like this:

It says: I address myself to you, a human individual called Peter (every individual is called by his name, in the passive sense, it is never he who provides his own name), in order to tell you that God exists and that you are answerable to Him. It adds: God addresses himself to you through my voice (Scripture having collected the Word of God, Tradition having transmitted it, Papal Infallibility fixing it for ever on 'nice' points). It says: this is who you are: you are Peter! This is your origin, you were created by God for all eternity, although you were born in the 1920th year of Our Lord! This is your place in the world! This is what you must do! By these means, if you observe the 'law of love' you will be saved, you, Peter, and will become part of the Glorious Body of Christ! Etc. . . . .

Now this is quite a familiar and banal discourse, but at the same time quite a surprising one.

Surprising because if we consider that religious ideology ̶i̶s̶ ̶i̶n̶d̶e̶e̶d̶ ̶a̶d̶d̶ressed to individuals,[19] in order to 'transform ̶t̶h̶e̶m̶ ̶i̶n̶t̶o̶ ̶s̶u̶b̶j̶ects', by interpellating the individual, Peter, ̶t̶o̶ ̶m̶a̶k̶e̶ him a subject, free to obey or disobey the ̶a̶p̶p̶e̶a̶ ̶G̶o̶d̶'s commandments; if it calls these individ-̶u̶a̶l̶s̶ ̶b̶y̶ ̶n̶a̶mes, thus recognizing that they are always-̶a̶l̶r̶e̶a̶d̶y̶ ̶i̶n̶t̶e̶r̶p̶e̶llated as subjects with a personal identity ̶(̶t̶o̶ ̶t̶h̶e̶ ̶e̶x̶t̶e̶n̶t̶ ̶t̶hat Pascal's Christ says: 'It is for you that I ̶h̶a̶v̶e̶ ̶s̶h̶e̶d̶ ̶t̶h̶i̶s̶ drop of my blood!'); if it interpellates them ̶i̶n̶ ̶s̶u̶c̶h̶ ̶a̶ ̶w̶a̶y̶ ̶t̶hat the subject responds: '*Yes, it really is me!*' ̶i̶f̶ ̶i̶t̶ ̶o̶b̶t̶a̶i̶n̶s̶ ̶f̶r̶om them the *recognition* that they really do ̶o̶c̶c̶u̶p̶y̶ ̶t̶h̶e̶ ̶p̶l̶a̶ce it designates for them as theirs in the world, a fixed residence: 'It really is me, I am here, a worker, a boss or a soldier!' in this vale of tears; if it obtains from them the recognition of a destination (eternal life or damnation) according to the respect or contempt they show to 'God's Commandments', Law become Love; – if everything does happen in this way (in the practices of the well-known rituals of baptism, confirmation, communion, confession and extreme unction, etc. . . .), we should note that all this 'procedure' to set up Christian religious subjects is dominated by a strange phenomenon: the fact that there can only be such a multitude of possible religious subjects on the absolute condition that there is a Unique, Absolute, *Other Subject*, i.e. God.

It is convenient to designate this new and remarkable Subject by writing Subject with a capital S to distinguish it from ordinary subjects, with a small s.

It then emerges that the interpellation of individuals as subjects presupposes the 'existence' of a Unique and central Other Subject, in whose Name the religious ideology

---

19. Although we know that the individual is always already a subject, we go on using this term, convenient because of the contrasting effect it produces.

s subjects. All this is clearly[20] ed the Scriptures. 'And it came l the Lord (Yahweh) spoke to ord cried to Moses, "Moses!" lly) I! I am Moses thy servant, speak and I shall listen!" And the Lord spoke to Moses and said to him, "*I am that I am*" '.

God thus defines himself as the Subject *par excellence*, he who is through himself and for himself ('I am that I am'), and he who interpellates his subject, the individual subjected to him by his very interpellation, i.e. the individual named Moses. And Moses, interpellated–called by his Name, having recognized that it 'really' was he who was called by God, recognizes that he is a subject, a subject *of* God, a subject subjected to God, *a subject through the Subject and subjected to the Subject.* The proof: he obeys him, and makes his people obey God's Commandments.

God is thus the Subject, and Moses and the innumerable subjects of God's people, the Subject's interlocutors-interpellates: his *mirrors*, his *reflections*. Were not men made *in the image* of God? As all theological reflection proves, whereas He 'could' perfectly well have done without men, God needs them, the Subject needs the subjects, just as men need God, the subjects need the Subject. Better: God needs men, the great Subject needs subjects, even in the terrible inversion of his image in them (when the subjects wallow in debauchery, i.e. sin).

Better: God duplicates himself and sends his Son to the Earth, as a mere subject 'forsaken' by him (the long complaint of the Garden of Olives which ends in the Crucifixion), subject but Subject, man but God, to do what prepares the way for the final Redemption, the Resurrection

20. I am quoting in a combined way, not to the letter but 'in spirit and truth'.

of Christ. God thus needs to 'make himself' a man, the Subject needs to become a subject, as if to show empirically, visibly to the eye, tangibly to the hands (see St Thomas) of the subjects, that, if they are subjects, subjected to the Subject, that is solely in order that finally, on Judgement Day, they will re-enter the Lord's Bosom, like Christ, i.e. re-enter the Subject.[21]

Let us decipher into theoretical language this wonderful necessity for the duplication of *the Subject into subjects* and of *the Subject itself into a subject-Subject*.

We observe that the structure of all ideology, interpellating individuals as subjects in the name of a Unique and Absolute Subject is *speculary*, i.e. a mirror-structure, and *doubly* speculary: this mirror duplication is constitutive of ideology and ensures its functioning. Which means that all ideology is *centred*, that the Absolute Subject occupies the unique place of the Centre, and interpellates around it the infinity of individuals into subjects in a double mirror-connexion such that it *subjects* the subjects to the Subject, while giving them in the Subject in which each subject can contemplate its own image (present and future) the *guarantee* that this really concerns them and Him, and that since everything takes place in the Family (the Holy Family: the Family is in essence Holy), 'God will *recognize* his own in it', i.e. those who have recognized God, and have recognized themselves in Him, will be saved.

Let me summarize what we have discovered about ideology in general.

The duplicate mirror-structure of ideology ensures simultaneously:

21. The dogma of the Trinity is precisely the theory of the duplication of the Subject (the Father) into a subject (the Son) and of their mirror-connexion (the Holy Spirit).

1. the interpellation of 'individuals' as subjects;

2. their subjection to the Subject;

3. the mutual recognition of subjects and Subject, the subjects' recognition of each other, and finally the subject's recognition of himself;[22]

4. the absolute guarantee that everything really is so, and that on condition that the subjects recognize what they are and behave accordingly, everything will be all right: Amen – '*So be it*'.

Result: caught in this quadruple system of interpellation as subjects, of subjection to the Subject, of universal recognition and of absolute guarantee, the subjects 'work', they 'work by themselves' in the vast majority of cases, with the exception of the 'bad subjects' who on occasion provoke the intervention of one of the detachments of the (repressive) State apparatus. But the vast majority of (good) subjects work all right 'all by themselves', i.e. by ideology (whose concrete forms are realized in the Ideological State Apparatuses). They are inserted into practices governed by the rituals of the ISAs. They 'recognize' the existing state of affairs (*das Bestehende*), that 'it really is true that it is so and not otherwise', and that they must be obedient to God, to their conscience, to the priest, to de Gaulle, to the boss, to the engineer, that thou shalt 'love thy neighbour as thyself', etc. Their concrete, material behaviour is simply the inscription in life of the admirable words of the prayer: '*Amen – So be it*'.

Yes, the subjects 'work by themselves'. The whole

22. Hegel is (unknowingly) an admirable 'theoretician' of ideology insofar as he is a 'theoretician' of Universal Recognition who unfortunately ends up in the ideology of Absolute Knowledge. Feuerbach is an astonishing 'theoretician' of the mirror connexion, who unfortunately ends up in the ideology of the Human Essence. To find the material with which to construct a theory of the guarantee, we must turn to Spinoza.

mystery of this effect lies in the first two moments of the quadruple system I have just discussed, or, if you prefer, in the ambiguity of the term *subject*. In the ordinary use of the term, subject in fact means: (1) a free subjectivity, a centre of initiatives, author of and responsible for its actions; (2) a subjected being, who submits to a higher authority, and is therefore stripped of all freedom except that of freely accepting his submission. This last note gives us the meaning of this ambiguity, which is merely a reflection of the effect which produces it: the individual is interpellated as a (*free*) *subject in order that he shall submit freely to the commandments of the Subject, i.e. in order that he shall* (*freely*) *accept his subjection*, i.e. in order that he shall make the gestures and actions of his subjection 'all by himself'. *There are no subjects except by and for their subjection.* That is why they 'work all by themselves'.

> *This sounds like hegemony: consenting to subjection.*

'*So be it! . . .*' This phrase which registers the effect to be obtained proves that it is not 'naturally' so ('naturally': outside the prayer, i.e. outside the ideological intervention). This phrase proves that it *has* to be so if things are to be what they must be, and let us let the words slip: if the *reproduction of the relations of production is to be assured*, even in the processes of production and circulation, every day, in the 'consciousness', i.e. in the attitudes of the individual-subjects occupying the posts which the socio-technical division of labour assigns to them in production, exploitation, repression, ideologization, scientific practice, etc. Indeed, what is really in question in this mechanism of the mirror recognition of the Subject and of the individuals interpellated as subjects, and of the guarantee given by the Subject to the subjects if they freely accept their subjection to the Subject's 'commandments'? The reality in question in this mechanism, the reality which is necessarily *ignored* (*méconnue*) in the very forms of recognition (ideology = misrecognition/ignorance) is indeed, in the last resort, the reproduction of the relations of production and of the relations deriving from them.

January–April 1969

P.S. If these few schematic theses allow me to illuminate certain aspects of the functioning of the Superstructure and its mode of intervention in the Infrastructure, they are obviously *abstract* and necessarily leave several important problems unanswered, which should be mentioned:

1. The problem of the *total process* of the realization of the reproduction of the relations of production.

As an element of this process, the ISAs *contribute* to this reproduction. But the point of view of their contribution alone is still an abstract one.

It is only within the processes of production and circulation that this reproduction is *realized*. It is realized by the mechanisms of those processes, in which the training of the workers is 'completed', their posts assigned them, etc. It is in the internal mechanisms of these processes that the effect of the different ideologies is felt (above all the effect of legal–ethical ideology).

But this point of view is still an abstract one. For in a class society the relations of production are relations of exploitation, and therefore relations between antagonistic classes. The reproduction of the relations of production, the ultimate aim of the ruling class, cannot therefore be a merely technical operation training and distributing individuals for the different posts in the 'technical division' of labour. In fact there is no 'technical division' of labour except in the ideology of the ruling class: every 'technical' division, every 'technical' organization of labour is the form and mask of a *social* (= class) division and organization of labour. The reproduction of the relations of production can therefore only be a class undertaking. It is realized through a class struggle which counterposes the ruling class and the exploited class.

The *total process* of the realization of the reproduction of the relations of production is therefore still abstract, insofar as it has not adopted the point of view of this class struggle. To adopt the point of view of reproduction is therefore, in the last instance, to adopt the point of view of the class struggle.

2. The problem of the class nature of the ideolog*ies* existing in a social formation.

The 'mechanism' of ideology *in general* is one thing. We have seen that it can be reduced to a few principles expressed in a few words (as 'poor' as those which, according to Marx, define production *in general*, or in Freud, define *the* unconscious *in general*). If there is any truth in it, this mechanism must be *abstract* with respect to every real ideological formation.

I have suggested that the ideologies were *realized* in institutions, in their rituals and their practices, in the ISAs. We have seen that on this basis they contribute to that form of class struggle, vital for the ruling class, the reproduction of the relations of production. But the point of view itself, however real, is still an abstract one.

In fact, the State and its Apparatuses only have meaning from the point of view of the class struggle, as an apparatus of class struggle ensuring class oppression and guaranteeing the conditions of exploitation and its reproduction. But there is no class struggle without antagonistic classes. Whoever says class struggle of the ruling class says resistance, revolt and class struggle of the ruled class.

That is why the ISAs are not the realization of ideology *in general*, nor even the conflict-free realization of the ideology of the ruling class. The ideology of the ruling class does not become the ruling ideology by the grace of God, nor even by virtue of the seizure of State power alone. It is by the installation of the ISAs in which this ideology is realized and realizes itself that it becomes the ruling ideology. But this installation is not achieved all by itself; on the contrary, it is the stake in a very bitter and continuous class struggle: first against the former ruling classes and their positions in the old and new ISAs, then against the exploited class.

But this point of view of the class struggle in the ISAs is still an abstract one. In fact, the class struggle in the ISAs is indeed an aspect of the class struggle, sometimes an important and symptomatic one: e.g. the anti-religious struggle in the eighteenth century, or the 'crisis' of the educational ISA in every capitalist country today. But the class struggles in the ISAs is only one aspect of a class struggle which goes beyond the ISAs. The ideology that a class in power makes the ruling ideology in its ISAs is indeed 'realized' in those ISAs, but it goes beyond them, for it comes from elsewhere. Similarly, the ideology that a ruled class manages to defend in and against such ISAs goes beyond them, for it comes from elsewhere.

It is only from the point of view of the classes, i.e. of the class struggle, that it is possible to explain the ideolog*ies* existing in a social formation. Not only is it from this starting-point that it is possible to explain the realization of the ruling ideology in the ISAs and of the forms of class struggle for which the ISAs are the seat and the stake. But it is also and above all from this starting-point that it is possible to understand the provenance of the ideologies which are realized in the ISAs and confront one another there. For if it is true that the ISAs represent the *form* in which the ideology of the ruling class must *necessarily* be realized, and the form in which the ideology of the ruled class must *necessarily* be measured and confronted, ideologies are not 'born' in the ISAs but from the social classes at grips in the class struggle: from their conditions of existence, their practices, their experience of the struggle, etc.

April 1970

Reply to
John Lewis

Foreword

The reader will find an article and a note here, dating from June 1972.

The article, 'Reply to John Lewis', appeared, translated by Grahame Lock, in two numbers of the theoretical and political journal of the Communist Party of Great Britain, *Marxism Today*, in October and November 1972.

'Reply': because, a few months earlier (in its January and February numbers of 1972), the same journal had published a long critical article by John Lewis (a British Communist philosopher known for his interventions in political-ideological questions) under the title: 'The Althusser Case'.

The present text of the *Reply to John Lewis* follows the English version of the article, except that I have made some corrections, added a few paragraphs for purposes of clarification, and also added a Remark.

To this text I have joined an unpublished *Note*, which was to have been part of my *Reply*, but which was cut to avoid extending the limits of an article which had already grown too long.

1 May 1973
L.A.

Reply to John Lewis
(Self-Criticism)

I.

I want to thank *Marxism Today* for having published John Lewis's article about the books I have written on Marxist philosophy: *For Marx* and *Reading Capital*, which appeared in France in 1965. He took care to treat me in a special way, in the way a medical specialist treats a patient. The whole family, as it were, together with his silent colleagues, stood motionless at the bedside, while Dr John Lewis leaned over to examine 'the Althusser case'.[1] A long wait. Then he made his diagnosis: the patient is suffering from an attack of severe 'dogmatism' – a 'mediaeval' variety. The prognosis is grave: the patient cannot last long.

It is an honour for this attention to be paid to me. But it is also an opportunity for me to clear up certain matters, twelve years after the event. For my first article [reprinted in *For Marx*], which was concerned with the question of the 'young Marx', actually appeared in 1960, and I am writing in 1972.

A good deal of water has flowed under the bridge of history since 1960. The Workers' Movement has lived through many important events: the heroic and victorious resistance of the

---

1. The title of John Lewis's article is *The Althusser Case*. Not surprisingly: in his conclusion, John Lewis compares Marxism to . . . medicine.

Vietnamese people against the most powerful imperialism in the world; the Proletarian Cultural Revolution in China (1966-69); the greatest workers' strike in world history (ten million workers on strike for a month) in May 1968 in France – a strike which was 'preceded' and 'accompanied' by a deep ideological revolt among French students and petty-bourgeois intellectuals; the occupation of Czechoslovakia by the armies of the other countries of the Warsaw Pact; the war in Ireland, etc. The Cultural Revolution, May 1968 and the occupation of Czechoslovakia have had political and ideological repercussions in the whole of the capitalist world.

With hindsight one can judge things better. Lenin used to say: the criterion of practice is only really valid if it bears on a 'process' which is of some length. With the help of the 'practical test' of the twelve, ten or even seven years which have passed since the original articles were written, one can look back and see more clearly whether one was right or wrong. It is really an excellent opportunity.

Just one small point in this connexion. John Lewis, in his article, never for one moment talks about this political history of the Workers' Movement. In *For Marx* – that is, in 1965 – I was already writing about Stalin, about the Twentieth Congress of the Soviet Communist Party, and about the split in the International Communist Movement. John Lewis, on the other hand, writes as if Stalin had never existed, as if the Twentieth Congress and the split in the International Communist Movement had never occurred, as if May 1968 had never taken place, nor the occupation of Czechoslovakia, nor the war in Ireland. John Lewis is a pure spirit; he prefers not to talk about such concrete things as politics.

When he talks about philosophy, he talks about philosophy. Just that. Full stop. It has to be said that this is precisely what the majority of so-called philosophy teachers do in our bourgeois society. The last thing they want to talk about is politics! They would rather talk about philosophy. Full stop. That is just why Lenin, quoting Dietzgen, called them 'graduated flunkies' of the bourgeois state. What a wretched sight they make! For *all* the great philosophers in history, since the time of Plato, even the great bourgeois philosophers – not only the materialists but even idealists like Hegel – have talked about politics. They more or less recognized that to do philosophy was to do politics in the field of theory. And they had the courage to do their politics openly, *to talk about politics*.

Heaven be thanked, John Lewis has changed all that. John Lewis is a Marxist and we are in 1972. He does not feel the need to talk about politics. Let someone work that one out.

But to *Marxism Today* I must express my thanks for giving an important place to a discussion about philosophy. It is quite correct to give it this important place. The point has been made not only by Engels and of course by Lenin, but by Stalin himself! And, as we know, it has also been made by Gramsci and by Mao: the working class *needs philosophy* in the class struggle. It needs not only the Marxist *science* of history (historical materialism), but also Marxist philosophy (dialectical materialism). Why?

I should like to reply by using a formula. I will take the (personal) risk of putting it this way: the reason is that *philosophy is, in the last instance,*[2] *class struggle in the field of theory.*[3]

2. N.B.: *in the last instance.* I do not want to be misunderstood. What I am saying is that philosophy is, in the last instance, class struggle in the field of theory. I am not saying that philosophy is *simply* class struggle in the field of theory.

3. This formula, which is extremely condensed, might mislead the reader. I would therefore like to add three points to help orient him. (1) Because of its abstraction, its rationality and its system, philosophy certainly figures 'in' the field of theory, in the neighbourhood of the sciences, with which it stands in a

All this is, as John Lewis would say, perfectly 'orthodox'. Engels, whom Lenin quotes on the point in *What is to be Done?* , wrote in 1874 in his Preface to *The Peasant War* that there are three forms of the class struggle. The class struggle has not only an economic form and a political form *but also* a theoretical form. Or, if you prefer: the same class struggle exists and must therefore be fought out by the proletariat in the economic field, in the political field *and in the theoretical field*, always under the leadership of its party. When it is fought out in the theoretical field, the concentrated class struggle is called philosophy.

Now some people will say that all this is nothing but words. But that is not true. These words are *weapons* in the class struggle in the field of theory, and since this is part of the class struggle as a whole, and since the highest form of the class struggle is the political class struggle, it follows that these words which are used in philosophy are weapons in the political struggle.

Lenin wrote that 'politics is economics in a concentrated

specific set of relations. But philosophy is not (a) science. (2) Unlike the sciences, philosophy has an especially intimate relation with the class tendency of the *ideologies*; these, in the last instance, are *practical* and do not belong to theory ('theoretical ideologies' are in the last instance 'detachments' of the practical ideologies in the theoretical field). (3) In all these formulations, the expression 'in the last instance' designates 'determination in the last instance', the principal aspect, the 'weak link' of *determination*: it therefore implies the existence of one or more secondary subordinate, overdetermined and overdetermining aspects – *other* aspects. Philosophy is therefore not simply class struggle in theory, and ideologies are not simply practical: but they are practical 'in the last instance'. Perhaps there has not always been a full understanding of the *theoretical* significance of Lenin's political thesis of the 'weak link'. It is not simply a question of choosing *the* 'weak link' from a number of pre-existing and already identified links: the chain is so made that the process must be reversed. In order to recognize and identify the other links of the chain, in their turn, one must *first* seize the chain by the 'weak link'.

form'. We can say: philosophy is, in the last instance,⁴ the *theoretical* concentrate of politics. This is a 'schematic' formula. No matter! It expresses its meaning quite well, and briefly.

Everything that happens in philosophy has, in the last instance, not only political consequences in theory, but also political consequences *in politics*: in the political class struggle.

We will show in a moment why that is so.

Of course, since I cite Engels and Lenin in support of my point, John Lewis will surely say, once again, that I am talking like 'the last champion of an orthodoxy in grave difficulties'.⁵ O.K.! I am the defender of orthodoxy, of that 'orthodoxy' which is called the theory of Marx and Lenin. Is this orthodoxy in 'grave difficulties'? Yes, it is and has been since it came to birth. And these grave difficulties are the difficulties posed by the threat of bourgeois ideology. John Lewis will say that I am 'crying in the wilderness'. Is that so? No, it is not!

For Communists, when they are Marxists, and Marxists when they are Communists, *never* cry in the wilderness. Even when they are practically alone.

Why? We shall see.

I therefore take my stand on this theoretical basis of Marxism—a basis which is 'orthodox' precisely in so far as it is in conformity with the theory of Marx and Lenin. And it is on this basis that I want to take issue both with John Lewis and with *my own* past errors, on the basis of the need to carry on the class struggle in the field of theory, as Engels and Lenin argued, and on the basis of the definition of philosophy which I am now proposing (in June, 1972): *philosophy is, in the last instance, class struggle in the field of theory.*

4. See note 2 above.
5. I cite the expressions of John Lewis himself.

I will therefore leave aside all the rather imprudent remarks, some of them 'psychological', which John Lewis thought it worth making at the end of his article, about Althusser's *whole style of life and writing*. John Lewis is for example very worried, very put out, quite upset – good 'humanist' that he is – by the fact that Althusser 'argues exhaustively and with an extreme dogmatism', in a way which makes him think not so much of the Scholastics, who were great philosophers of the Middle Ages, but of the *schoolmen*, commentators of commentators, erudite splitters of philosophical hairs, who could not rise above the level of quotation. Thank you! But really, this kind of argument has no place in a debate between Communists in the journal of a Communist Party. I will not follow John Lewis onto this ground.

I approach John Lewis as a comrade, as a militant of a fraternal party: the Communist Party of Great Britain.

I will try to speak plainly and clearly, in a way that can be understood by all our comrades.

So as not to make my reply too long, I will only take up those theoretical questions which are most important, politically speaking, for us today, in 1972.

II.

To understand my reply, the reader must obviously know what John Lewis, in his 'radical' critique of my 'philosophical writings', essentially holds against me.

In a few words, we can sum this up as follows.
John Lewis holds:

1. that I do not understand Marx's *philosophy*;

2. that I do not understand the history of the *formation* of Marx's thought.

In short, his reproach is that I do not understand *Marxist theory*.

That is his right.

I will consider these two points in succession.

III.

First Point: *Althusser does not understand Marx's philosophy*.

To demonstrate this point, John Lewis employs a very simple method. First he sets out Marx's *real* philosophy, which is Marx as he understands him. Then, beside this, he puts Althusser's interpretation. You just have to compare them, it seems, to see the difference!

Well, let us follow our guide to Marxist philosophy and see how John Lewis sums up his own view of Marx. He does it in three formulae, which I will call three *Theses*.[6]

1. *Thesis no. 1*. 'It is man who makes history'.
John Lewis's argument: no need of argument, since it is obvious, it is quite evident, everyone knows it.
John Lewis's example: revolution. It is man who makes revolution.

2. *Thesis no. 2*. 'Man makes history by remaking existing history, by "transcending", through the "negation of the negation", already made history.'
John Lewis's argument: since it is man who makes history, it follows that in order to make history man must transform the history which he has already made (since it is man who has made history). To transform what one has already made is to 'transcend' it, to negate what exists. And since what

6. In a *Philosophy Course for Scientists* (1967, to be published), I proposed the following definition: 'Philosophy states propositions which are *Theses*'. (It therefore differs from the sciences. 'A science states propositions which are Demonstrations')

exists is the history which man has already made, it is already negated history. To make history is therefore 'to negate the negation', and so on without end.

John Lewis's example: revolution. To make revolution, man 'transcends' ('negates') existing history, itself the 'negation' of the history which preceded it, etc.

3. *Thesis no. 3.* 'Man only knows what he himself does.' *John Lewis's argument*. no argument, probably because of lack of space. So let us work one out for him. He could have taken the case of science and said that the scientist 'only knows what he himself does' because he is the one who has to work out his proof, either by experment or by demonstration (mathematics).

John Lewis's example: no example. So let us provide one. John Lewis could have taken *history* as an example: man's knowledge of history comes from the fact that he is the one who makes it. This is like the Thesis of Giambattista Vico: *verum factum.*[7]

These then are the three Theses which sum up John Lewis's idea of Marx's philosophy:

Thesis no. 1: It is man who makes history.

Thesis no. 2: Man makes history by transcending history.

Thesis no. 3: Man only knows what he himself does.

This is all very simple. Everyone 'understands' the words involved: *man, make, history, know*. There is only one word which is a bit complicated, a 'philosopher's' word: 'transcendence', or 'negation of the negation'. But if he wanted to, John Lewis could say the same thing more simply. Instead of saying: man makes history, in transcending it, by the 'negation of the negation', he could say that man makes history by 'transforming' it, etc. Wouldn't that be more simple?

---

7. 'What is true is what has been done.' Marx cites Vico in *Capital*, in connexion with the history of technology.

But a little difficulty still remains. When John Lewis says that it is man who makes history, everyone understands. Or rather, everyone thinks he understands. But when it is a question of going a bit further in the explanation, when John Lewis honestly asks himself the question: '*what* is it that man *does* when he makes history?', then you realize that a nasty problem appears just when everything seemed simple, that there is a nasty obscurity just in the place where everything seemed clear.

What was obscure? The little word *make*, in the Thesis that 'it is man who makes history'. What can this little word *make* possibly mean, when we are talking about *history*? Because when you say: 'I made a mistake' or 'I made a trip around the world', or when a carpenter says: 'I made a table', etc., everyone knows what the term 'make' means. The sense of the word changes according to the expression, but in each case we can easily explain what it means.

For example, when a carpenter 'makes' a table, that means he *constructs* it. But to *make* history? What can that mean? And the *man* who makes history, do you know that individual, that 'species of individual', as Hegel used to say?

So John Lewis sets to work. He does not try to avoid the problem: he confronts it. And he explains the thing. He tells us: to 'make', in the case of history, that means to 'transcend' (negation of the negation), that means to transform the raw material of existing history by going beyond it. So far, so good.

But the carpenter who 'makes' a table, he has a piece of 'raw material' in front of him too: the wood. And he transforms the wood into a table. But John Lewis would never say that the carpenter 'transcends' the wood in order to 'make' a table out of it. And he is right. For if he said that, the first carpenter who came along, and all the other carpenters and all the other working people in the world would send him packing with his 'transcendence'. John Lewis uses the term 'transcendence' (negation of the negation) *only* for history. Why? We have to work out the answer, for John Lewis himself does not provide any explanation.

In my opinion, John Lewis holds on to his 'transcendence' for the following reason: because the raw material of history *is already history*. The carpenter's raw material is *wood*. But the carpenter who 'makes' the table would never say that *he was the one who 'made'* the wood, because he knows very well that it is nature which produces the wood. Before a tree can be cut up and sold as planks, it first has to have grown somewhere in the forest, whether in the same country or thousands of miles away on the other side of the equator.

Now, for John Lewis it is man who *has made* the history with which *he makes* history. In history man produces everything: the result, the product of his 'labour', is history: but so is the *raw material* that he transforms. Aristotle said that man is a two-legged, reasoning, speaking, political animal. Franklin, quoted by Marx in *Capital*, said that man is a 'tool-making' animal. John Lewis says that man is not only a tool-making animal, but an animal which makes history, in the strong sense, because he *makes everything*. He 'makes' the raw material. He makes the instruments of production. (John Lewis says nothing about these – and for good reason! Because otherwise he would have to talk about the *class struggle*, and his 'man who makes history' would disappear in one flash, together with his whole system.) And he makes the final product: history.

Do you know of any being under the sun endowed with such a power? Yes – there does exist such a being in the tradition of human culture: *God*. Only *God* 'makes' the raw material with which he 'makes' the world. But there is a very important difference. John Lewis's God is not outside of the world: the man-god who creates history is not outside of history – he is *inside*. This is something infinitely more complicated! And it is just because John Lewis's little human god – man – is *inside* history ('*en situation*', as Jean-Paul Sartre used to say) that Lewis does not endow him with a power of absolute creation (when ones creates everything it is relatively easy: there are no limitations!) but with something even more stupefying – the power of 'transcendence', of being able to progress by indefinitely *negating-superseding* the constraints of the history *in which* he lives, the power to transcend history by *human liberty*.[8]

John Lewis's man is a little lay god. Like every living being he is 'up to his neck' in reality, but endowed with the prodigious power of being able at any moment to step outside of that reality, of being able to change its character. A little Sartrian god, always '*en situation*' in history, endowed with the amazing power of 'transcending' every situation, of resolving all the difficulties which history presents, and of going forward towards the golden future of the human, socialist revolution: man is an essentially revolutionary animal because he is a *free* animal.

Please excuse all this if you are not a philosopher. We philosophers are well acquainted with this kind of argument. And we Communist philosophers know that this old tune in philosophy has always had its politicla consequences.

The first people who talked about 'transcendence' in philosophy were the idealist-religious philosophers of Plato's school: the Platonic and neo-Platonic philosophers. They had an urgent need of the category of 'transcendence' in

8. I do not know John Lewis's personal philosophical history. But I am not sticking my neck out much in betting that he has a weakness for Jean-Paul Sartre. Lewis's 'Marxist Philosophy' in fact bears a remarkable resemblance to a copy of Sartrian existentialism, in a slightly Hegelianized form, no doubt designed to make it more acceptable to Communist readers.

order to be able to construct their philosophical or religious theology, and this theology was then the official philosophy of the slave state. Later, in the Middle Ages, the Augustinian and Thomist theologians took up the same category again and used it in systems whose function was to serve the interests of the Church and feudal state. (The Church is a State Apparatus, and the number one Ideological State Apparatus of the feudal state.) Is there any need to say more?

Much later, with the rise of the bourgeoisie, the notion of 'transcendence' received, in Hegelian philosophy, a new function: the same category, but 'wrapped' in the veil of the 'negation of the negation'. This time is served the bourgeois state. It was quite simply the *philosophical name* for *bourgeois liberty*. It was then revolutionary in relation to the philosophical systems of feudal 'transcendence'. But it was *one hundred per cent bourgeois*, and it stays that way.

Since that time, Jean-Paul Sartre has taken up the same idea once more, in his theory of man *'en situation'*: the *petty-bourgeois* version of *bourgeois liberty*. And this is to cite only one example, for Sartre is not alone – 'transcendence', in its authoritarian or eschatological form, is still flourishing today among large numbers of theologians, some reactionary, some very progressive, from Germany and Holland to Spain and Latin America. The bourgeois no longer has the same need to believe – and anyway has for the thirty years since 1940 no longer been able to believe – that his liberty is all-embracing. But the petty-bourgeois intellectual: he is quite a different kind of animal! The more *his* liberty is crushed and denied by the development of imperialist capitalism, the more he exalts the power of that liberty ('tanscendence', 'negation of the negation'). An *isolated* petty-bourgeois can protest: he does not get very far. When the petty-bourgeois *masses* revolt, however, they get much further. But their revolt is still limited by the objective conditions of the class struggle, whether it is helped or hindered by them. It is here that petty-bourgeois *liberty* meets *necessity*.

John Lewis now, in 1972, takes up the old arguments in his turn, in the theoretical journal of the British Communist Party. He can, if I may say so, rest assured: he is not 'crying in the wilderness'! He is not the only person to take up this theme. He is in the company of many Communists. Everyone knows that. But why should it be that since the nineteen-sixties many Communists have been resurrecting this worn-out philosophy of petty-bourgeois liberty, while still claiming to be *Marxists*?

We shall see.

IV.

But first, I shall follow the procedure used by John Lewis. I shall compare his 'Marxist' Theses with the Theses of Marxist-Leninist philosophy. And everyone will be able to compare and judge for himself.

I will go over the points in John Lewis's order. That way things will be clearer. I am making an enormous concession to him by taking his order, because his order is idealist. But we will do him the favour.

To understand what follows, note that in the case of each Thesis (1,2,3) I begin by repeating Lewis's Thesis and then state the Marxist-Leninist Thesis.

1. THESIS NO. 1

John Lewis: 'It is *man* who makes history'.
Marxism-Leninism: 'It is the *masses* which make history'.

What is this 'man' who 'makes' history? A mystery.[9]

What are the 'masses' which make history? In a class society they are the *exploited* masses, that is, the exploited social classes, social strata and social categories, grouped around the exploited class *capable* of uniting them in a movement against the dominant classes which hold state power.

The exploited class capable of doing this is not always *the most* exploited class, or *the most* wretched social 'stratum'.

In Antiquity, for example, it was not the slaves (except in a few periods – Spartacus) who 'made' history in the strong, political sense of the term, but the most exploited classes among the 'free' men (at Rome, the urban or rural 'plebs').[10]

In the same way, under capitalism the 'lumpenproletariat', as Marx called it, groups together the most wretched of men, the 'lazarus-layers of the working class'.[11] But it is around the proletariat (the class which is exploited in capitalist *production*) that you will find grouped the masses which 'make history', which are going to 'make history' – that is, who are going to make the revolution which will break out in the 'weakest link' of the world imperialist chain.

9. For us, struggling under the rule of the bourgeoisie, 'man' who makes history is a mystery. But this 'mystery' did have a sense when the revolutionary bourgeoisie was struggling against the feudal regime which was then dominant. To proclaim *at that time*, as the great bourgeois Humanists did, that it is *man* who makes history, was to struggle, *from the bourgeois point of view* (which was then revolutionary), against the religious Thesis of feudal ideology: it is *God* who makes history. But we are no longer in their situation. Moreover, the bourgeois point of view has always been idealist as far as history is concerned.

10. It is not certain – here I shall have to bow to the judgement of Marxist historians – that the slave class did not, in spite of everything, quietly but genuinely 'make history'. The transition from the small-property slave system to the large-scale system at Rome is perhaps significant here.

11. *Capital*, Part VII, Ch. XXV, sec.4. Excluded from production, without fixed work or completely unemployed, (often) in the street, the sub-proetarians are part of the reserve army, the army of unemployed, which capitalism uses *against* the workers.

Against John Lewis's Thesis – it is man who makes history – Marxism-Leninism has always opposed the Thesis: it is the masses which make history. The masses can be defined. In capitalism, *the masses* does not mean '*the mass*' of aristocrats of the 'intelligentsia', or of the ideologists of fascism; it means the set of exploited *classes*, strata and categories grouped around *the class* which is exploited *in large scale production*, the only class which is capable of uniting them and directing their action against the bourgeois state: the proletariat. Compare this with Lewis's Thesis.

2. THESIS NO. 2

John Lewis: 'Man makes history by "transcending" history'. *Marxism-Leninism*: 'The class struggle is the motor of history' (Thesis of the *Communist Manifesto*, 1847).

Here things become extremely interesting. Because Marxism-Leninism blows up John Lewis's whole philosophical system. How?

John Lewis said: it is man who makes history. To which Marxism-Leninism replied: it is *the masses*.

But if we said no more, if we went no further, we would give the impression that Marxism-Leninism gives a *different* reply to the *same* question. That question being: *who makes history?* This question therefore supposes that history is the result of the action of (what is done by) a *subject* (who)? For John Lewis, the subject is 'man'. Does Marxism-Leninism propose a *different subject*, the masses?

Yes and no. When we started to sketch out a definition of the masses, when we talked about this idea of the masses, we saw that the whole thing was rather complicated. The masses are actually *several* social classes, social strata and social categories, grouped *together* in a way which is both complex and *changing* (the positions of the different classes and strata, and of the fractions of classes within classes, *change* in the course of the revolutionary process itself). And we are dealing with huge numbers: in France or Britain, for example, with tens of millions of people, in China with hundreds of millions! Let us do no more here than ask the simple question: can we still talk about a 'subject', identifiable by the *unity* of its 'personality'? Compared with John Lewis's subject, 'man', as simple and neat as you can imagine, the masses, considered as a subject, pose very exacting problems of identity and identification. You cannot hold such a 'subject' in your hand, you cannot point to it. A subject is a being about which we can say: 'that's it!'. How do we do that when the masses are supposed to be the 'subject'; how can we say: 'that's it'?

It is precisely the Thesis of the *Communist Manifesto* – 'the class struggle is the motor of history' – that *displaces the question*, that brings the problem into the open, that shows us how to pose it properly and therefore how to solve it. It is the masses which 'make' history, but 'it is the class struggle which is the motor of history'. To John Lewis's question: 'how does man make history?', Marxism-Leninism replies by replacing his idealist philosophical categories with categories of a quite different kind.

The question is no longer posed in terms of 'man'. That much we know. But in the proposition that 'the class struggle is the motor of history', the question of 'making' history is also eliminated. It is no longer a question of *who* makes history.

Marxism-Leninism tells us something quite different: that it is the *class struggle* (new concept) which is the *motor* (new concept) of history, it is the class struggle which moves history, which advances it: and brings about revolutions. This Thesis is of very great importance, because *it puts the class struggle in the front rank.*

In the preceding Thesis: 'it is the masses which make history', the accent was put (1) on the exploited classes grouped around the class capable of uniting them, and (2) on their power to carry through a revolutionary transformation of history. It was therefore the masses which were put in the front rank.

In the Thesis taken from the *Communist Manifesto*, what is put in the front rank is no longer the exploited classes, etc., but the class struggle. This Thesis must be recognized as decisive for Marxism-Leninism. It draws a radical demarcation line between revolutionaries and reformists. Here I have to simplfy things very much, but I do not think that I am betraying the essential point.

For *reformists* (even if they call themselves Marxists) it is not the class struggle which is in the front rank: it is simply the classes. Let us take a simple example, and suppose that we are dealing with just two classes. For reformists these classes exist *before* the class struggle, a bit like two football teams exist, separately, before the match. Each class exists in its own camp, lives according to its particular conditions of existence. One class may be exploiting another, but for reformism that is not the same thing as class struggle. One day the two classes come up against one another and come into conflict. It is only then that the class struggle begins. They begin a hand-to-hand battle, the battle becomes acute, and finally the exploited class defeats its enemy (that is revolution), or loses (that is counter-revolution). However you turn the thing around, you will always find the same idea here: the classes exist *before* the class struggle, *independently* of the class struggle. The class struggle only exists *after-wards*.[12]

Revolutionaries, on the other hand, consider that it is impossible to separate the classes from class struggle. The class struggle and the existence of classes are one and the same thing. In order for there to be classes in a 'society', the society has to be *divided* into classes: this division does not come *later in the story*; it is the exploitation of one class by another, it is therefore the class struggle, which constitutes the division into classes. For exploitation is already class struggle. You must therefore begin with the class struggle if you want to understand class division, the existence and nature of classes. *The class struggle must be put in the front rank*.

But that means that our Thesis 1 (*it is the masses which make history*) must be subordinated to Thesis 2 (*the class struggle is the motor of history*). That means that the revolutionary power of the masses comes precisely from the *class struggle*. And that means that it is not enough, if you want to understand what is happening in the world, just to look at the exploited classes. You also have to look at the exploiting classes. Better, you have to go beyond the football match

12. To clarify this point, this reformist 'position' must be related to its bourgeois origins. In his letter to Weydemeyer (5 March 1852), Marx wrote: 'No credit is due to me for discovering the existence of classes in modern society, nor yet the struggle between them. Long before me bourgeois historians had described the historical development of this struggle of the classes, and bourgeois economists the economic anatomy of the classes'. The thesis of the recognition of *the existence of social classes*, and of *the resulting class struggle* is not proper to Marxism-Leninism: for it puts the classes in the front rank, and the class struggle in the second. *In this form* it is a bourgeois thesis, which reformism naturally feeds on. The Marxist-Leninist thesis, on the other hand, puts the *class struggle* in the front rank. Philosophically, that means: it affirms the *primacy of contradiction* over the *terms* of the contradiction. The class struggle is not a product of the existence of classes which exist *previous* (in law and in fact) to the struggle: the class struggle is the historical form of the *contradiction* (internal to a mode of production) which *divides* the classes into classes.

idea, the idea of two antagonistic groups of classes, to examine the basis of the existence *not only* of classes but also of the antagonism between classes: that is, the *class struggle*. Absolute primacy of the class struggle (Marx, Lenin). Never forget the class struggle (Mao).

But beware of idealism! The class struggle does not go on in the air, or on something like a football pitch. It is rooted in the mode of production and exploitation in a given class society. You therefore have to consider the *material basis* of the class struggle, that is, the material *existence* of the class struggle. This, in the last instance, is the unity of the relations of production and the productive forces *under* the relations of production of a given mode of production, in a concrete historical social formation. This materiality, in the last instance, is at the same time the 'base' (*Basis*: Marx) of the class struggle, and its material existence; because exploitation takes place in production, and it is exploitation which is at the root of the antagonism between the classes and of the class struggle. It is this profound truth which Marxism-Leninism expresses in the well-known Thesis of class struggle in the infrastructure, in the 'economy', in class exploitation – and in the Thesis that *all the forms of the class struggle are rooted in economic class struggle*. It is on this condition that the revolutionary thesis of the primacy of the class struggle is a materialist one.

When that is clear, the question of the 'subject' of history disappears. History is an immense *natural-human* system in movement, and the motor of history is class struggle. History is a process, and a *process without a subject*.[13] The question

13. I put this idea forward in a study called 'Marx and Lenin before Hegel' (February 1968), published with *Lenin and Philosophy*, Maspero, Paris, 1972 [English translation in Louis Althusser, *Politics and History*, NLB, 1972]. For more details, see below the *Remark on the Category: 'Process without a Subject or Goal(s)*.

about how 'man makes history' disappears altogether. Marxist theory rejects it once and for all; it sends it back to its birthplace: bourgeois ideology.

And with it disappears the 'necessity' of the concept of 'transcendence' and of its subject, man.

That does not mean that Marxism-Leninism *loses sight* for one moment of real men. Quite the contrary! It is precisely in order to *see* them as they are and to free them from class exploitation that Marxism-Leninism brings about this revolution, getting rid of the bourgeois ideology of 'man' as the subject of history, *getting rid of the fetishism of 'man'*.

Some people will be annoyed that I dare to speak about the fetishism of 'man'. I mean those people who interpret Marx's chapter in *Capital* on 'The Fetishism of Commodities' in a particular way, drawing two necessarily complementary idealist conclusions: the condemnation of 'reification'[14] and the exaltation of the *person*. (But the pair of notions *person/thing* is at the root of every bourgeois ideology! *Social* relations are however not, except for the law and for bourgeois legal ideology, 'relations between persons'!). Yet it is the same mechanism of social illusion which is at work – when you start to think that a social relation is the natural quality, the natural attribute of a *substance* or a *subject*. Value is one example: this social relation 'appears' in bourgeois ideology as the natural quality, the natural attribute of the commodity or of money. The class struggle is another example: this social relation 'appears' in bourgeois ideology as the natural quality, the natural attribute of 'man' (liberty, transcendence). In both cases, the social relation is 'conjured away': the commodity or gold have *natural* value; 'man' is *by nature* free, *by nature* he makes history.

14. Transformation into a *thing* (*res*) of everything which is *human*, that is, a *non-thing* (man = non-thing = Person).

If John Lewis's 'man' disappears, that does not mean that real men disappear. It simply means that, for Marxism-Leninism, they are something quite different from copies (multiplied at will) of the original bourgeois image of 'man', a free subject by nature. Have the warnings of Marx been heeded? 'My analytical method *does not start from man*, but from the economically given social period' (*Notes on Adolph Wagner's 'Textbook'*). 'Society *is not composed of individuals*' (*Grundrisse*).

One thing is certain: one cannot *begin* with man, because that would be to begin with a bourgeois idea of 'man', and because the idea of *beginning with* man, in other words the idea of an absolute point of departure (= of an 'essence') belongs to bourgeois philosophy. This idea of 'man' as a starting-point, an absolute point of departure, is the basis of all bourgeois ideology; it is the soul of the great Classical Political Economy itself. 'Man' is a myth[15] of bourgeois ideology: Marxism-Leninism cannot *start* from 'man'. It starts 'from the economically given social period'; and, at the end of its analysis, when it 'arrives', *it may find real men*. These men are thus the *point of arrival* of an analysis which starts from the social relations of the existing mode of production, from class relations, and from the class struggle. These men are quite different men from the 'man' of bourgeois ideology.

'Society is not *composed of individuals*', says Marx. He is right: society is not a 'combination', an 'addition' of individuals. What constitutes society is the system of its social relations in which *its* individuals live, work and struggle. He is right: society is not made up of individuals in general, in the abstract, just so many copies of 'man'. Because each

15. The word 'man' is not simply a word. It is the place which it occupies and the function which it performs in bourgeois ideology and philosophy that gives it its *sense*.

society has *its own* individuals, historically and socially determined. The slave-individual is not the serf-individual nor the proletarian-individual, and the same goes for the individual of each corresponding ruling class. In the same way, we must say that even a class is not 'composed' of individuals in general: each class has *its own* individuals, fashioned in their individuality by their conditions of life, of work, of exploitation and of struggle – by the relations of the class struggle. In their mass, real men are what class conditions make of them. These conditions do not depend on bourgeois 'human nature': liberty. On the contrary: the liberties of men, including the forms and limits of these liberties, and including their will to struggle, depend on these conditions.

If the question of 'man' as 'subject of history' disappears, that does not mean that the question of *political action* disappears. Quite the contrary! This political action is actually given its strength by the critique of the bourgeois fetishism of 'man': it is forced to follow the conditions of the class struggle. For class struggle is not an individual struggle, but an *organized* mass struggle for the conquest and revolutionary transformation of state power and social relations. Nor does it mean that the question of the revolutionary *party* disappears – because without it the conquest of state power by the exploited masses, led by the proletariat, is impossible. But it does mean that the 'role of the individual in history', the existence, the nature, the practice and the objectives of the revolutionary party are not determined by the omnipotence of 'transcendence', that is, the liberty of 'man', but by quite different conditions: by the state of the class struggle, by the state of the labour movement, by the ideology of the labour movement (petty-bourgeois or proletarian), and by its relation to Marxist theory, by its mass line and by its mass work.

3. THESIS NO. 3

John Lewis: 'Man only knows what he himself *does*'. *Marxism-Leninism*: 'One can only know what *exists*' (ce qui *est*).

I am deliberately putting these propositions into such direct opposition: so that everyone can see the difference.

For John Lewis, 'man' only knows what he 'does'. For dialectical materialism, the philosophy of Marxism-Leninism, one can only know what *exists*. This is the fundamental Thesis of materialism: 'the primacy of being over thought!'.

This Thesis is at one and the same time a Thesis about existence, about materiality and about objectivity. It says that one can only know what *exists*; that the principle of all existence is *materiality*; and that all existence is *objective*, that is, 'prior' to the 'subjectivity' which knows it, and independent of that subjectivity.

One can only know what *exists*. This Thesis, difficult to understand, and easy to misrepresent, *is the basis* of all Marxist Theses about knowledge. Marx and Lenin never denied the 'activity' of thought, the work of scientific experiment, from the natural sciences to the science of history, whose 'laboratory' is the class struggle. Indeed, they insisted on this activity. They even, now and again, said and repeated that certain idealist philosophers (Hegel, for example) had understood this 'activity' better, though in 'mystified' forms, than certain non-dialectical materialist philosophers. This is where we get to the dialectical Theses of Marxist philosophy, But – and this is where it differs fundamentally from John Lewis – *Marxism-Leninism has always subordinated the dialectical Theses to the materialist Theses*. Take the famous Thesis of the primacy of practice over theory: it has no sense unless it is subordinated to the Thesis of the primacy of being over thought. Otherwise it falls into subjectivism, pragmatism and historicism. It is certainly thanks to practice (of which scientific practice is the most developed form) that one can know what exists: primacy of practice over theory. But in practice one only ever knows what exists: primacy of being over thought.

'One can only know what exists.' As far as nature is concerned, there ought not to be much problem: who could claim that 'man' had 'made' the natural world which he knows? Only idealists, or rather only that crazy species of idealists who attribute God's omnipotence to man. Even idealists are not normally so stupid.

But what about history? We know that the Thesis: 'it is man who makes history' has, literally, no sense. Yet a trace of the illusion still remains in the idea that history is *easier* to understand than nature because it is completely 'human'. That is Giambattista Vico's idea.

Well, Marxism-Leninism is categorical on this point: history is as difficult to understand as nature. Or, rather, it is even more difficult to understand. Why? Because 'the masses' do not have the same *direct practical* relation with history as they have with nature (in productive work), because they are always *separated* from history by *the illusion that they understand it*. Each ruling exploiting class offers them 'its own' explanation of history, in the form of its ideology, which is dominant, which serves its class interests, cements its unity, and maintains the masses under its exploitation.

Look at the Middle Ages: the Church and its ideologists offered all its flock – that is to say, primarily the exploited masses, but also the feudal class and itself – a very simple and clear explanation of history. History is made by God, and obeys the laws, that is, the ends, of Providence. An explanation for the 'masses'.

Look at the eighteenth century in France. The situation is different: the bourgeoisie is not yet in power, it is critical and revolutionary. And it offers everyone (without distinction of class! not only to the bourgeoisie and its allies, but also to the masses it exploits) a 'clear' explanation of history: history is moved by Reason, and it obeys the laws or follows the ends of Truth, Reason and Liberty. An explanation for the 'masses'.

If history is difficult to explain scientifically, it is because *between* real history and men there is always a screen, a separation: *a class ideology of history* in which the human masses 'spontaneously' believe: because this ideology is pumped into them by the ruling or ascending class, and serves it in its exploitation. In the eighteenth century the bourgeoisie is already an exploiting class.

To succeed in piercing this ideological and idealist 'smoke-screen' of the ruling classes, the special circumstances of the first half of the nineteenth century were required: the experience of the class struggles following the French Revolution (1789, 1830) and the first proletarian class struggles, *plus* English political economy, *plus* French socialism. The result of the conjuncture of all these circumstances was Marx's discovery. He was the first to open up the 'Continent of History' to scientific knowledge.

But in history, as in nature, one can only know what *exists*. The fact that, in order to get to know what really does *exist*, an enormous amount of scientific work and gigantic practical struggles were necessary, does not disprove the point. One can only know what *exists*, even if this is *changing*, under the effect of the material dialectic of the class struggle, even if what *exists* is only known on condition that it is *transformed*.

But we must go further. You will notice that I said that the Marxist-Leninist Thesis is not 'man can only know what exists', but: '*one* can only know what exists'.[16] Here too the

16. I wrote 'one can only know what exists', in order not to complicate

term 'man' has disappeared. We are forced to say in this connexion that scientific history, like all history, is a *process without a subject*, and that scientific knowledge (even when it is the work of a particular individual scientist, etc.) is actually the historical result of a process which has no real subject or goal(s). That is how it is with Marxist science. It was Marx who 'discovered' it, but as the result of a dialectical process, combining German philosophy, English political economy and French socialism, the whole thing based on the struggles between the bourgeoisie and the working class. All Communists know that.

Scientists, in general, do not know it. But if they are prepared to, and if they have enough knowledge of the history of the sciences, Communists can help scientists (including natural scientists and mathematicians) to understand its truth. Because all scientific knowledge, in every field, really is the result of a process without any subject or goal(s). A startling Thesis, one which is doubtless difficult to understand. But it can give us 'insights' of a certain importance, not only into scientific work, but also into the political struggle.

V.

For all these philosophical Theses, these philosophical positions (Thesis = position) produce *effects* in the social practices. Among them, effects in political practice and scientific practice.

But we have to generalise: it is not only the philosophical Thesis which we have already discussed that produce these

---

things. But it might be objected that this impersonal 'one' bears the traces of 'man'. Strictly speaking, we should write: 'only what exists *can be known*'.

effects, but *all* philosophical Theses. Because if there is one idea which is popular today – even among some Marxists – it is the idea of philosophy as pure contemplation, pure *disinterested* speculation. Now this dominant idea is actually the very self-interested representation of idealism created by idealism itself. It is a mystification of idealism, necessary to idealism, to represent philosophy as purely speculative, as a pure revelation of Being, Origin and Meaning. Even speculative ideologies, even philosophies which content themselves with '*interpreting the world*', are in fact active and practical: their (hidden) goal is to act on the world, on all the social practices, on their domains and their 'hierarchy' – even if only in order to 'place them under a spell', to sanctify or modify them, in order to preserve or reform 'the existing state of things' against social, political and ideological revolutions or the ideological repercussions of the great scientific discoveries. 'Speculative' philosophies have a political *interest* in making believe that they are *disinterested* or that they are only 'moral', and not really practical and political: this in order to gain their practical ends, in the shadow of the ruling power which they support with their arguments. Whether this strategy is 'conscious' and deliberate or 'unconscious' means little: we know that it is not consciousness which is the motor of history, even in philosophy.

You will remember the definition of philosophy which I proposed above. We can apply this definition to every philosophy: philosophy is, in the last instance, class struggle in the field of theory.

In philosophy is *class struggle* in theory, if it depends in the last instance on politics, then – as philosophy – it has political effects: in political practice, in the *way* in which 'the concrete analysis of the concrete situation' is made, in which 'the concrete analysis of the concrete situation' is made, in which the mass line is defined, and in which mass work is carried out. But if it is class struggle in the field of *theory*, then it has theoretical effects: in the sciences, and also within the field of the ideologies. If it is *class struggle in the field of theory*, it has effects on the union of theory and practice: on the *way* in which that union is conceived and realized. It therefore has effects, of course, not only in political practice and scientific practice, but also in *every* social practice,[17] from the 'struggle for production' (Mao) to art, etc.[18]

But I cannot deal with everything here. I will just say that philosophy, as class struggle in the field of theory, has two main effects: in politics and in the sciences, in political practice and in scientific practice. Every Communist knows that, or ought to know it, because Marxism-Leninism has never ceased to repeat it and argue for it.

So let us now set out our schematic 'proof', by comparing John Lewis's Theses with the Theses of Marxism-Leninism. That will allow us to show a little more clearly how philosophy 'functions'.

John Lewis's Thesis: 'It is man who makes history'.

17. John Lewis is right to criticize me on this point: philosophy is not only 'concerned' with politics and the sciences, but with *all* social practices.

18. How are these effects produced? This question is very important. Let us limit ourselves to the following comment: (1) Philosophy is not Absolute Knowledge; it is neither the Science of Sciences, nor the Science of Practices. Which means: it does not possess the Absolute Truth, either about any science or about any practice. In particular, it does not possess the Absolute Truth about, nor power over, political practice. On the contrary, Marxism affirms the primacy of politics over philosophy. (2) But philosophy is nevertheless not 'the servant of politics', as philosophy was once 'the servant of theology': because of its position *in theory*, and of its *'relative autonomy'*. (3) What is *at stake* in philosophy is the real problems of the social practices. As philosophy is not (a) science, its relation to these problems is not a *technical relation of application*. Philosophy does not provide formulae to be 'applied' to problems: philosophy cannot be applied. Philosophy works in a quite different way: by modifying the *position* of the problems, by modifying the *relation* between the practices and their object. I limit myself to stating the principle, which would require a long explanation.

Thesis of Marxism-Leninism: 'It is the masses which make history; the class struggle is the motor of history'.

Let us look at the *effects* of these Theses.

1. EFFECTS IN THE FIELD OF SCIENCE

When someone, in 1972, defends the idealist Thesis that 'it is man who makes history', what effect does that have as far as the *science* of history is concerned? More precisely: can one make use of it to produce scientific discoveries?

It is a very regrettable fact, no doubt, but it is in fact no use at all from this point of view. John Lewis himself does not get anything out of it which might help us to see how the class struggle works. You might say that he didn't have the space in a single article. That is perhaps true. So let us turn to his (unavowed) Master, Jean-Paul Sartre, to the philosopher of 'human liberty', of man-projecting-himself-into-the-future (John Lewis's transcendence), of man '*en situation*' who 'transcends' his place in the world by the liberty of the 'project'. This philosopher (who deserves the praise given by Marx to Rousseau: that he never compromised with the powers-that-be) has written two enormous books – *Being and Nothingness* (1939), and the *Critique of Dialectical Reason* (1960), the latter devoted to proposing a philosophy for Marxism. More than two thousand pages. Now, what did Sartre get out of the Thesis: 'it is man who makes history'?[19] What did it contribute to the science of history? Did the ingenious developments of the Sartrian positions finally permit the production of a few pieces of scientific knowledge about the economy, the class struggle,

19. Sartre's Theses are obviously more subtle. But John Lewis's version of them, schematic and poor as it is, is not basically unfaithful to them.

the state, the proletariat, ideologies, etc. – knowledge which might help us to understand history, to act in history? We have, unfortunately, reason to doubt it.

But then someone is going to say: here is an example which proves just the opposite of your Thesis about the effects of philosophy, because, as you recognize, this 'humanist' philosophy has *no effect at all* on scientific knowledge. Sorry! I claim that Theses like those defended by John Lewis and Jean-Paul Sartre really do have such an effect, even though it is a *negative* one: because they 'prevent' the development of existing scientific knowledge. Lenin said the same of the idealist philosophies of his own time. These Theses are an obstacle to the development of knowledge. Instead of helping it to progress, they hold it back. More precisely, they drag knowledge back to the state it was in *before* the scientific discoveries made by Marx and Lenin. They take us back to a pre-scientific 'philosophy of history'.

It is not the first time that this has happened in the history of humanity. For example, half a century after Galileo – that is, half a century after physics had been founded as a *science* – there were still philosophers who defended Aristotelian 'physics'! They attacked Galileo's discoveries and wanted to drag knowledge of the natural world back to its pre-scientific Aristotelian state. There are no longer any Aristotelian 'physicists'; but the same process can be observed in other fields. For example: there are anti-Freudian 'psychologists'. And there are anti-Marxist philosophers of history, who carry on as if Marx had never existed, or had never founded a science. They may be personally honest. They may even, like Sartre, want to 'help' Marxism and psychoanalysis. But it is not their intentions that count. What count are the real *effects* of their philosphies in these sciences. The fact is that although he comes *after* Marx and Freud, Sartre is, paradoxically, in many respects a pre-Marxist and pre-Freudian ideologian from the philosophical point of view. Instead of helping to build on the scientific discoveries of Marx and Freud, he makes a spectacular appearance in the ranks of those whose work does more to hinder Marxist research than to help it.

That is how, in the end, philosophy 'works' in the sciences. *Either* it helps them to produce new scientific knowledge, *or* it tries to wipe out these advances and drag humanity back to a time when the sciences did not exist. Philosophy therefore works in the sciences in a progressive or retrogressive way. Strictly speaking, we should say that it *tends* to act in one way or another – for every philosophy is always contra-dictory.[20]

You can see what is at stake. It is not enough to say that what John Lewis or Sartre says does not help us to produce any scientific knowledge of history. It is not even enough to argue that what they say represents an 'epistemological obstacle' (to use Bachelard's term). We are forced to say that their Thesis produces or can produce effects which are extremely harmful to scientific knowledge, retrogressive effects, because instead of helping us, in 1972, to understand the great scientific treasure that we possess in the knowledge given us by Marx, and to develop it,[21] it goes back to zero. It takes us back to the good old days of Descartes, or Kant and Fichte, of Hegel and Feuerbach, to the time *before* Marx's discovery, before his 'epistemological break'. This idealist Thesis mixes everything up, and thus it paralyses revolution-ary philosophers, theoreticians and militants. It disarms

20. There is no absolutely *pure* idealist or materialist philosophy, even if only because every philosophy must, in order to take up its own theoretical class posi-tions, *surround* those of its principal adversary. But one must learn to recognize the *dominant tendency* which results from its contradictions, and masks them.

21. Lenin said: Marx has given us the 'corner-stones' of a theory which we must 'develop in every direction'.

them, because in effect it deprives them of an irreplaceable weapon: the objective knowledge of the conditions, mechanisms and forms of the class struggle.

If you now look at the Marxist-Leninist Theses – 'it is the masses which make history', 'the class struggle is the motor of history' – the contrast is striking. These Theses do not paralyse research: they are *on the side of* a scientific understanding of history. They do not wipe out the science of history founded by Marx – for these two philosophical Theses are at the same time proven propositions of the science of history, of historical materialism.[22]

These Theses, then, take account of the *existence* of the science of history. But at the same time they help the working out of *new* concepts, of new scientific discoveries. For example, they lead us to define the masses which make history – in class terms. For example, they lead us to define the form of union between the classes which make up the masses. As far as the class struggle under capitalism is concerned, they put the question of taking state power, the long transition (to communism) and the proletariat in the forefront. For example, they cause us to conceive the unity of the class struggle and of class division, and all their consequences, *in the material forms* of exploitation and of the division and organization of labour, and therefore to study and come to understand these forms. For example, they lead us to define the proletariat as a class whose conditions of exploitation render it capable of directing the struggle of all the oppressed and exploited classes, and to understand the proletarian class struggle as a form of class struggle without precedent in history, inaugurating a 'new practice of politics',[23] which is

22. The fact that scientific propositions may *also*, in the context of a philosophical debate, 'function philosophically' is worthy of thought.

23. Cf. Etienne Balibar, 'La Rectification du *Manifeste communiste*', *La Pensée*, August 1972.

the secret of many still enigmatic or evaded questions.

The theoretical consequences of these questions are obvious. They force us above all to break with the bourgeois – that is, the *economist* conception – of political economy ('criticized' as such by Marx in *Capital*), with the bourgeois conception of the state, of politics, of ideology, of culture, etc. They prepare the ground for new research and new discoveries, some of which might cause a few surprises.

On the one side, then, we have idealist philosophical Theses which have theoretically retrograde effects on the science of history. On the other side we have materialist philosophical Theses which have theoretically progressive effects in the existing fields of the Marxist science of history, and which can have revolutionary effects in those fields which have not yet been really grappled with by the science of history (for example in the history of the sciences, of art, of philosophy, etc.).

This is what is at stake as far as the class struggle in the theoretical field is concerned.

2. POLITICAL EFFECTS

I think that, as far as political effects are concerned, things are rather clear.

How could one carry on the class struggle on the basis of the philosophical Thesis: 'it is man who makes history'? It might be said that this Thesis is useful in fighting against a certain conception of 'History': history in submission to the decisions of a Deity or to the Ends of Providence. But, speaking seriously, that is no longer the problem!

It might be said that this Thesis serves *everyone*, without distinction, whether he be a capitalist, a petty-bourgeois or a worker, because these are all 'men'. But that is not true. It serves *those* whose interest it is to talk about 'man' *and not* about the masses, about 'man' *and not* about classes and the class struggle. It serves the bourgeoisie, above all; and it also serves the petty-bourgeoisie. In his *Critique of the Gotha Programme*, Marx wrote: 'The bourgeois have very good grounds for falsely ascribing *supernatural creative power* to [human] labour'.[24] Why? Because by making 'men' think that 'labour is the source of all wealth and all culture', the bourgeoisie can keep quiet about the power of '*nature*', about the decisive importance of the *natural, material conditions* of human labour. And why does the bourgeoisie want to keep quiet about the natural-material conditions of labour? Because *it controls them*. The bourgeoisie knows what it is doing.

If the workers are told that 'it is men who make history', you do not have to be a great thinker to see that, sooner or later, that helps to disorient or disarm them. It tends to make them think that they are all-powerful as men, whereas in fact they are disarmed as workers in the face of the power which is really in command: that of the bourgeoisie, which controls the material conditions (the means of production) and the political conditions (the state) determining history. The humanist line turns the workers away from the class struggle, prevents them from making use of the only power they possess: that of their *organization as a class* and their *class organizations* (the trade unions, the party), by which they wage *their* class struggle.

On the one hand, therefore, we have a philosophical Thesis

24. Marx's emphasis. Marx was therefore criticizing the formula of the social-ist John Lewises of his time, inscribed in the Unity Programme of the German Social-Democratic Party and Lassalle's Party: '*Labour is the source of all wealth and all culture*'.

which, directly or indirectly, serves the political interests of the bourgeoisie, even inside the labour movement (that is called reformism), and even within 'Marxist' theory (that is called revisionism), with all the consequent political effects.

On the other hand we have Theses which directly help the working class to understand its role, its conditions of existence, of exploitation and of struggle, which help it to create organizations which will lead the struggle of all exploited people to seize state power from the bourgeoisie.

Need I say more?

None of this is affected by the fact that these bourgeois or petty-bourgeois Theses are defended, in 1972, by a militant of a Communist Party. Read chapter 3 of the *Communist Manifesto*. You will see that in 1847 Marx distinguished three kinds of socialism: reactionary (feudal, petty-bourgeois, *humanist*[25]) socialism, conservative or bourgeois socialism, and critical-utopian socialism and communism. You have the choice! Read the great polemical writings of Engels and Lenin about the influence of bourgeois ideology in the workers' parties (reformism, revisionism). You have the choice!

What we want to know now is how, after so many solemn warnings and so many testing experiences, it is possible for a Communist – John Lewis – to present his 'Theses' as Marxist.

We shall see.

VI.

So as not to hold things up, I will be brief in dealing with John Lewis's second reproach: *that 'Althusser' does not understand anything of the history of the formation of Marx's thought.*

25. Then called 'True' or 'German' socialism.

Here I must make my self-criticism, and give way to John Lewis on one precise point.

In my first essays, I suggested that after the 'epistemological break' of 1845 (after the discovery by which Marx founded the science of history) the philosophical categories of *alienation and the negation of the negation* (among others) disappear. John Lewis replies that this is not true. And he is right. You certainly do find these concepts (directly or indirectly) in the *German Ideology*, in the *Grundrisse* (two texts which Marx never published) and also, though more rarely (alienation) or much more rarely (negation of the negation: only one explicit appearance) in *Capital*.

On the other hand John Lewis would have a hard job finding these concepts in the *Communist Manifesto*, in the *Poverty of Philosophy*, in *Wage Labour and Capital*, in his *Contribution to the Critique of Political Economy*, in the *Critique of the Gotha Programme* or in the *Notes on Wagner's Textbook*. And this is to cite only some of Marx's texts. As far as the political texts are concerned – and this of course is equally true of the texts of Lenin,[26] Gramsci or Mao – well, he can always try!

But in any case, formally speaking John Lewis is right. And so, even if his argument in fact depends on leaving aside all the texts which could bother him, I must reply.

Here, in a few words, is my reply.

1. If you look at the whole of Marx's work, there is no doubt that there does exist a 'break' of some kind in 1845. Marx *says so* himself. But of course no one should be believed simply on his word, not even Marx. You have to judge on the evidence. Nevertheless, the whole work of Marx shows him to be right on this point. In 1845 Marx *began* to lay down the foundations of a science which did not exist before

---

26. He can certainly cite Engel's use of the negation of the negation in *Anti-Dühring* – which can be found in Lenin's *What the 'Friends of the People' Are*. But it is a rather 'peculiar' defence: an anti-Hegelian one.

he came along: the science of history. And in order to do that he set out a number of new concepts which cannot be found anywhere in his humanist works of youth: *mode of production, productive forces, relations of production, infrastructure-superstructure, ideologies*, etc. No one can deny that.

If John Lewis still doubts the reality of this 'break', or rather – since the 'break' is only the effect – of this *irruption* of a new science in a still 'ideological' or pre-scientific universe, he should compare two judgements made by Marx on Feuerbach and Proudhon.

Feuerbach is described in the *1844 Manuscripts* as a philosopher who has made extraordinary discoveries, who has discovered both the basis and the principle of the critique of political economy! But a year later, in the *Theses on Feuerbach*, and in the *German Ideology*, he is object of an all-out attack. After that he simply disappears.

Proudhon is described in the *Holy Family* (end of 1844) as someone who 'does not simply *write* in the interest of the proletariat, but is himself a proletarian, a worker. His work is *a scientific manifesto of the French proletariat*.'[27] But in 1847, in the *Poverty of Philosophy*, he gets a hiding from which he will never recover. After that he simply disappears.

If, as John Lewis says, *nothing* really happened in 1845, and if everything that I have said about the 'epistemological break' is 'a complete myth', then I'll be hung for it.

2. So something *irreversible* really does start in 1845: the 'epistemological break' is a point of *no return*. Something begins which will have no end.[28] A 'continuing break', I wrote, the beginning of a long period of work, as in every other science. And although the way ahead is open, it is difficult

27. *The Holy Family*, English translation, Moscow 1956.
28. Lenin speaking of the study of imperialism: 'This study is only beginning and *it is without an end*, by its very nature, like science in general'. (*The Collapse of the Second International*.)

and sometimes even dramatic, marked by events – theoretical events (additions, rectifications, corrections) – which concern the scientific knowledge of a particular object: the conditions, the mechanisms and the forms of the class struggle. In simpler terms, the science of history.

We can say, then, that this science does not emerge, ready-made, from Marx's head. It merely *has its beginning* in 1845, and has not yet got rid of all its past – of all the ideological and philosophical prehistory out of which it has emerged. There is nothing astonishing in the fact that for some time it continues to contain ideological notions or philosophical categories which it will later get rid of.

We can also say: look at Marx's texts, look at the birth and development of his scientific concepts, and – since John Lewis insists on talking about them – you will at the same time see the gradual disappearance of these two philosophical categories inherited from the past and still subsisting as remnants, known as *alienation* and the *negation of the negation*. Now in fact, the more we advance in time, the more these categories disappear. *Capital* speaks only once of the negation of the negation in explicit terms. It is true that Marx several times uses the *term* 'alienation'. But all that disappears in Marx's later texts and in Lenin. Completely.[29] We could therefore simply say: what is important is the *tendency*: and Marx's scientific work does *tend* to get rid of these philosophical categories.

3. But this is not sufficient. And here is my self-criticism.

I was not attentive enough to the *fact* which John Lewis points out, that is, to the fact of the continuing presence of the said philosophical categories *after* the 'epistemological

29. One really must be short of arguments to have to use, as a proof of Lenin's 'humanist philosophy', a few lines from *The German Ideology* (1844) which Lenin copied into his notebook! John Lewis is obviously not worried about gaining the reputation of 'schoolman' himself.

break'. And that was because I identified the 'epistemological (= *scientific*) break' with Marx's philosophical revolution. More precisely, I did not separate Marx's philosophical revolution from the 'epistemological break', and I therefore talked about philosophy as if it were science, and quite logically wrote that in 1845 made a *double* break, scientific *and* philosophical.

That was a mistake. It is an example of the *theoreticist* (= rationalist-speculative) deviation which I denounced in the brief self-criticism contained in the Preface to the Italian edition of *Reading Capital* (1967), reproduced in the English edition.[30] Very schematically, this mistake consists in thinking that philosophy is a *science*, and that, like every science, it has: (1) an *object*; (2) a *beginning* (the 'epistemological break' occurs at the moment when it *looms up* in the pre-scientific, ideological cultural universe); and (3) a *history* (comparable to the history of a science). This theoreticist error found its clearest and purest expression in my formula: Philosophy is 'Theory of theoretical practice'.[31]

Since that time, I have begun to 'put things right'. In a philosophy course for scientists, dating from 1967, and then in *Lenin and Philosophy* (February 1968), I put forward other propositions:

1. Philosophy is not (a) science.

2. Philosophy has no object, in the sense in which a science has an object.

3. Philosophy has no history, in the sense in which a science has a history.

30. And in the edition of *Reading Capital* published in the Petite Collection Maspero, 1968, vol. 1.

31. The corrections which I later made to this formula (for example: Philosophy is 'Theory of theoretical practice in its distinction from the *other* practices', or 'Theory of the processes of the production of knowledge', or '. . . of the material and social conditions of the processes of production of knowledge', etc., in *For Marx* and *Reading Capital*) do not touch the root of this error.

4. Philosophy is politics in the field of theory.

What are the consequences.?

1. It is impossible to reduce philosophy to science, and it is impossible to reduce Marx's philosophical revolution to the 'epistemological break'.

2. Marx's philosophical revolution preceded Marx's 'epistemological break'. It *made the break possible*.

One can of course put forward serious arguments to the effect that there is a sense in which philosophy, as Hegel said, and as I repeated in *Lenin and Philosophy*, always 'lags behind' science or the sciences. But from another point of view, which is important here, one has to say the opposite, and argue that in the history of Marx's thought the scientific breakthrough is based on the philosophical revolution, which gives the breakthrough its form: that of a *revolutionary science*.

In the case of other sciences, we often lack evidence and proof of what happened. But in the case of Marx, we are able to say that while both the philosophical revolution and the epistemological break take place 'at the same time', the scientific break is based on the philosophical revolution.

In practical terms, that means the following. The young Marx, born of a good bourgeois family in the Rhineland, entered public life as editor of a liberal newspaper of the same land. That was in 1841. A young and brilliant intellectual, he was, within three or four years, to undergo an astonishing evolution *in politics*. He was to pass from radical bourgeois liberalism (1841-42) to petty-bourgeois communism (1843-44), then to proletarian communism (1844-45). These are incontestable facts. But parallel to this political evolution you can observe an evolution in philosophy. *In philosophy*, over the same period, the young Marx was to pass from a position of subjective neo-Hegelianism (of a Kant-Fichte type) to theoretical humanism (Feuerbach), before rejecting this to pass over to a philosophy which would no longer merely 'interpret' the world: a completely new, materialist-revolutionary philosophy.

If you now compare Marx's political evolution with his philosophical evolution, you will see:

1. that his philosophical evolution is based on his political evolution; and

2. that his scientific discovery (the 'break') is based on his philosophical evolution.

That means, in practice, that it is because the young Marx had 'settled accounts' with his previous philosophical consciousness (1845), because he had finally abandoned his bourgeois liberal and petty-bourgeois revolutionary positions to adopt (even if only in principle, at a moment when he was letting go the ropes) new revolutionary-proletarian class positions in theory, it was because of all this that he was able to lay down the foundations of the scientific theory of history as history of the class struggle. *In principle*: because the process of recognizing and occupying these new positions in theory needed time. Time, in a ceaseless struggle to contain the pressure of bourgeois philosophy.

4. On the basis of these points it should be possible to account for the intermittent survival of categories like those of *alienation* and of the *negation of the negation*. Note that I talk about intermittent survival. For alongside their *tendency* to disappear in Marx's work, considered as a whole, there is a strange phenomenon which must be accounted for: their total disappearance in certain works, then their *subsequent* reappearance. For example, the two categories in question are absent from the *Communist Manifesto* as well as from the *Poverty of Philosophy* (published by Marx in 1847). They seem to be hidden in his *Contribution to the Critique of Political Economy* (which he published in 1859). But there are many references to alienation in the *Grundrisse* (preparatory notes

made by Marx in the years 1857-58, and which he *did not publish*). We know because of a letter sent to Engels, that Marx had 'by chance' re-read Hegel's *Logic* in 1858 and had been fascinated by it. In *Capital* (1867) alienation comes up again, but much more rarely, and the negation of the negation appears just once. And so on.[32]

However that might be, and without anticipating other studies which must be made if the *contradictory* dialectic of Marx's development and the elaboration of his work is to be understood, one fact is clear. The Marxist science of history did not progress in a simple straight line, according to the classic *rationalist* scheme, without problems or internal conflicts, and under its own power, from the moment of the 'point of no return' – the 'epistemological break'. There certainly is a 'point of no return', *but* in order not to be forced to retreat, it is necessary to advance – and to advance, how many difficulties and struggles there are! For if it is true that Marx had to pass over to proletarian class positions in theory in order to found the science of history, he did not make that leap all at once, once and for all, for ever. It was

32. One must be careful with philosophical categories taken *one by one*: for it is less their name than their function in the theoretical apparatus in which they operate that decides their 'nature'. Is *a particular* category idealist or materialist? In many cases we have to reply with Marx's answer: 'That depends'. But there are limit-cases. For example, I do not really see that one can expect anything positive from the category of the *negation of the negation*, which contains within it an irreparable idealist charge. On the other hand it seems to me that the category of alienation can render *provisional* services, given a double and absolute condition: (1) that it be 'cut' from every philosophy of 'reification' (or of fetishism, or of self-objectivization) which is only an anthropological variant of idealism; and (2) that alienation is understood as *secondary* to the concept of exploitation. On this double condition, the category of alienation can, *in the first instance* (since it disappears in the final result) help to avoid a purely *economic*, that is, economist conception *of surplus-value*: it can help to introduce the idea that, in exploitation, *surplus-value is inseparable from the concrete and material forms in which it is extorted*. A number of texts from the *Grundrisse* and from *Capital* go, in my opinion, in this sense. But I know that others go in a different and much more ambiguous sense.

necessary to *work out* these positions, to take them up over and against the enemy. The philosophical battle continued within Marx himself, in his work: around the principles and concepts of the new revolutionary science, which was one of the stakes of the battle. Marxist science only gained its ground little by little, in theoretical struggle (class struggle in theory), in close and constant relation to the class struggle in the wider sense. This struggle lasted all of Marx's life. It continued after his death, in the labour movement, and it is still going on today. A struggle without an end.

It is therefore possible to understand, at least in principle, the partial disappearance and reappearance of certain categories in Marx's work as indicative of survivals of old ideas or attempts to work out new ones, of advances and retreats in the long dual struggle to take up class positions in theoretical work and to found the science of history.

When I said that it was the 'epistemological break' which was primary, and when I said that it was at the same time a *philosophical* 'break', I therefore made two mistakes. In the case of Marx it is the philosophical revolution which is *primary* – and this revolution is not a 'break'. The theoretical terminology itself is important here: if one can legitimately keep the term 'break' to denote the beginning of the science of history, the clear effect of its irruption in the cultural universe, the point of no return, one cannot employ the same term in talking about philosophy. In the history of philosophy, as in very long periods of the class struggle, one cannot really talk about a point of no return. So I shall use the term: philosophical 'revolution' (in the strong sense in Marx's case). This expression is more correct: for – to evoke once again the experiences and terms of the class struggle – we all know that a revolution is always open to attacks, to retreats and reverses, and even to the risk of counter-revolution.

Nothing in philosophy is *radically* new, for the old Theses, taken up again in new form, survive and return in a new philosophy. Nor is anything ever settled *definitively*: there is always the struggle of antagonistic tendencies, there are always 'come-backs', and the oldest philosophies are always ready to mount an offensive disguised in modern – even the most revolutionary – trappings. Why?

Because philosophy is, in the last instance, class struggle in the field of theory. Because the revolutionary classes are always opposed by the old conservative and reactionary ruling classes, who will never give up their ambition for revenge, even when they no longer hold state power. According to the state of affairs, these classes will either defend their power or, if they have lost power, they will try to regain it, using among other things the arguments of such-and-such a philosophy: that which serves them best politically and ideo-logically, even if it comes out of the depths of history. It only has to be done up a bit and given a modern coat of paint. Philosophical Theses, in the end, have 'no age'. That is the sense in which I took up Marx's comment in the *German Ideology* that 'philosophy has no history'.

In practice, when the state of the class struggle enables it to put on enough pressure, bourgeois ideology can penetrate Marxism itself. The class struggle in the field of theory is not just a phrase: it is a reality, a terrible reality. Without under-standing that, it is impossible to understand either the dramatic history of the formation of Marx's thought or the 'grave difficulties' which even today, in 1972, weigh on the 'orthodoxy' defended by a certain number of Communists.

The dramatic history of Marx and of his thought can be reduced, if we follow John Lewis, to a peaceful and problem-free university career! A certain Marx appears on the literary and philosophical scene. Quite naturally, he begins to talk about politics in the *Communist Manifesto*, then about econo-mics in *Capital*. He founds and directs the First International, opposes the insurrection in Paris, then in the space of two months, takes a firm stand on the side of the Paris Commune. He wages a battle to the death against the anarchists and followers of Proudhon, etc., etc. All this without the hint of a problem, of a drama, aside from all the assaults of the struggle, with no regard to the difficulties, the questions, all the torments of the search for 'truth' in that struggle itself. Like a good bourgeois intellectual, as well installed in his thought as he is in the comfort of his existence, Marx, in this view, *always thought the same thing*, without any revolution or 'break' in his thinking: he always taught that 'man makes history', by the 'negation of the negation', etc. I think I am justified in saying here that only someone who has no experience of the class struggle, including class struggle in the field of theory – or even simply of the way in which scientific research is done – could argue such nonsense, and thus insult the life and sufferings not only of Marx himself but of all Communists (and also of all those scientists who succeed in *finding something out*). Now, not only did Marx 'find something out' (and at what risk, and of what importance!), but he was also a *leader* of the labour movement for thirty-five years. He always did his thinking and his 'investigating' *in and through the struggle*.

The whole history of the labour movement is marked by endless crises, dramas and struggles. There is no need for me to go over them here. But as far as philosophy is concerned, we ought at least to mention the great struggles of Engels and Lenin against the intervention of the idealism of Dühring and of Bernstein, both of them declared neo-Kantians and humanists, whose theoretical revisionism covered their political reformism and political revisionism.

John Lewis would do well to re-read the first pages of *What is to be Done*? In this text a petty-bourgeois intellectual named Lenin is defending Marx's 'orthodoxy', which is 'in grave difficulties'. With 'extreme dogmatism' (I use Lewis's terms). Yes, Lenin declared himself proud to be attacked as a 'dogmatist' by the international coalition of 'critical' revisionists, with the 'English Fabians' and 'French Ministerialists' at their head! (I am quoting Lenin.) Yes, Lenin declared himself proud to defend this old problem-ridden 'orthodoxy', the orthodoxy of Marx's teaching. Yes, he thought it was 'in grave difficulties'. The cause: reformism and revisionism!

Some Communists today, are thinking and doing the same. There certainly are not too many of them.

That is how things are. Why? We shall see.

VII.

We have to answer two questions.

1. Why are there Communists like John Lewis (and there are quite a lot of them) who, in 1972, can openly argue in Communist journals for a philosophy which they call Marxist, but which is in fact simply a variant of bourgeois idealism?

2. Why are the Communist philosophers who defend Marx's philosophy so few in number?

To answer these two questions, which are really one and the same, we must – all apologies to John Lewis – briefly enter the field of political history.

I have made the basic points in *For Marx*. But John Lewis does not seem to have read the political pages of *For Marx*. John Lewis is a pure spirit.

And yet I was rather clear in explaining that the articles collected in *For Marx* had to be considered as a philosophical intervention in a political and ideological conjuncture dominated by the Twentieth Congress and the 'split' in the

International Communist Movement.[33] The fact that I was able to make such an intervention is a consequence of the Twentieth Congress.

Before the Twentieth Congress it was actually not possible for a Communist philosopher, certainly in France, to publish texts which would be (at least to some extent!) relevant to politics, which would be something other than a pragmatist commentary on consecrated formulae. That is the good side of the Twentieth Congress, for which we must be grateful. From that time on it was possible to publish such texts. The French Party, to take only one example, explicitly recognized (at the Argenteuil Central Committee meeting in 1966) the right of party members to carry out and publish their philosophical research.

But the 'criticism of Stalin's errors' was formulated at the Twentieth Congress in terms such that there inevitably followed what we must call an unleashing of *bourgeois* ideological and philosophical themes within the Communist Parties themselves. This was the case above all among Communist intellectuals, but it also touched certain leaders and even certain leaderships. Why?

Because the 'criticism of Stalin's errors' (some of which – and rather a lot – turned out to be crimes) was made in a non-Marxist way.

The Twentieth Congress criticized and denounced the 'cult of personality' (the cult in general, personality in general . . .) and summed up Stalin's 'errors' in the concept of 'violation of Socialist *legality*'. The Twentieth Congress therefore limited itself to denouncing certain *facts* about what went on in the *legal superstructure*, without relating them – as every Marxist analysis must do – firstly, to the rest of the Soviet superstructure (above all, the state and party), and secondly, to the infrastructure, namely the relations of

33. Cf. the Introduction to *For Marx*.

production, class relations and the forms of the class struggle in the USSR.[34]

Instead of relating the 'violations of socialist legality' to: 1. the state, *plus* the party, and: 2. the class struggle, the Twentieth Congress instead related them to . . . the 'cult of personality'. That is, it related them to a concept which, as I pointed out in *For Marx*, cannot be 'found' in Marxist theory. I now venture to say that it can perfectly well be 'found' elsewhere: in *bourgeois* philosophy and psycho-sociological ideology.

If you take Communist philosophers and other Communist 'intellectuals' and set them officially on a bourgeois ideological and philosophical line, in order to 'criticize' a regime under which they (among others) have suffered deeply, you must not be surprised when the same Communist philosophers and intellectuals quite naturally take the road of bourgeois philosophy. It has been opened up right in front of them! You must not be surprised when they make up their own little bourgeois Marxist philosophy of the Rights of Man, exalting Man and his Rights, the first of which is *liberty*, whose reverse is *alienation*. It is quite natural for them to lean on Marx's early works – that is what they are there for – and then on humanism in all its forms! Shall it be Garaudy's socialist humanism, the pure humanism of John

---

34. Lenin: 'In theory there is undoubtedly a certain period of transition between capitalism and communism. It must necessarily combine the traits or particularities of these two economic structures of society. This transitory period can only be a period of struggle between the death agony of capitalism and the birth of communism, or, in other terms: between vanquished, but not yet eliminated capitalism, and already born, but still weak communism. [. . .] Classes remain and will remain in the era of the dictatorship of the proletariat. [. . .] Classes remain, but each class has undergone a change in the era of the dictatorship of the proletariat; the relations between the classes have also changed. The class struggle does not disappear under the dictatorship of the proletariat, it simply takes other forms' (*Economics and Politics in the Era of the Dictatorship of the Proletariat*).

Lewis, the 'true' or 'real' socialism of others, or even (why not?) 'scientific' humanism itself? Between these different varieties of the philosophy of human *liberty*, each philosopher can of course *freely* take his choice! All that is perfectly normal.

Having said that, we must add that it is important not to mix things up which, politically speaking, ought not to be confused, things which are quite different from one another. The humanist reactions of western Communist theoreticians, and even of some from eastern Europe, are one thing. It would however be an extremely serious political mistake, for example, to claim to judge and condemn – on account of an adjective ('human') – something like the slogan *'socialism with a human face'*, a slogan under which the Czech masses let everyone know – even if the form was sometimes confused – about their class and national grievances and aspirations. It would be an extremely serious political mistake to confuse this national mass movement, this important historical fact, with the humanist pedantry of our western, sometimes Communist philosophers (or of such-and-such a philosopher of eastern Europe). There were intellectuals in the Czech national mass movement, but it was not a 'movement of intellectuals'. What the Czech people wanted was *socialism*, and not humanism. It wanted a socialism whose *face* (not the *body*: the body does not figure in the formula) would not be disfigured by practices unworthy both of itself (the Czech people: a people of a high political culture) and of socialism. A socialism with a human face. The adjective is in the right place. The national mass movement of the Czech people, even if it is no longer to be heard of (and the struggle is nevertheless still going on) merits the respect and support of all Communists. Exactly as the 'humanist' philosophies of western intellectuals (at ease in their academic chairs or wherever), the philosphies of 'Marxist humanism', whether they are called 'true' or 'scientific', merit the criticism of all Communists.

It is for all the reasons outlined above, then, that there are cases like John Lewis in the western Communist Parties – and that there are rather a lot of them.

It is for the same reasons that, in these parties, there exists a certain number of Communist philosophers who are fighting against a certain current – and that there are rather few of them.

And it is for these reasons – directly political reasons – that I want to repeat my thanks to *Marxism Today*, journal of the Communist Party of Great Britain, for accepting to publish my reply.

Paris, July 4 1972

Note on 'The Critique of the Personality Cult'

Not for one moment does the idea strike John Lewis that 'philosophy is as close to politics as the lips are to the teeth', that, 'in the last instance', what is at stake – indirectly, but also very directly – where *philosophical Theses* are concerned is always a number of *political* problems or arguments of real history, and that every philosophical text (including his own) is 'in the last instance' *also* a political intervention in the theoretical conjuncture *as well as*, through one of its effects, today the main effect, a theoretical intervention in the political conjuncture. Not for a moment does the idea strike him of wondering about the political conjuncture in which my texts (and his own) were written, about what theoretical-political 'effects' I had in mind when thinking them out and publishing them, about the framework of theoretical argument and political conflicts in which the enterprise was undertaken, or about the reactions it caused.

I am not expecting John Lewis to have a detailed knowledge of French political and philosophical history, of the struggle of ideas (even unimportant or erroneous ideas) within the French Communist Party since the war, and especially between 1960 and 1965. But all the same! Communists have a history in common: a long, difficult, happy and unhappy history, one which to a large extent in linked to the Third International, itself dominated since the thirties by Stalin's political 'line' and leadership. We have a common past, as Communists, in the Popular Fronts, the Spanish War, the Second War and the anti-fascist resistance, and the Chinese Revolution. But we also have Lysenko's 'science', which was no more than ideology, and a few formulae and slogans which were claimed to be 'scientific' but were no more than 'ideological', and which concealed very strange practices.[1] We all share, as Communists, a past which includes Khrushchev's 'criticism of the personality cult' at the Twentieth Congress of the Soviet Party, and the ordeal of the split in the International Communist Movement. We have the Chinese Cultural Revolution in common, whatever we think of it, and May '68 in France. A few ups and downs, in short, from which one ought to be able to abstract so as to 'talk philosophy' between Communists in 1972 . . .

It is not too serious a matter. Because one day we really shall have to try and call things by their *name*, and to do that, as Marxists, we have to look for that *name*; I mean the right *concept* (even if we have to do it while we advance), so that we can come to understand our own history. Our history is not like a peaceful stream flowing between secure banks, its course marked out in advance, any more than Marx's own history was, or the tragic and glorious history of the first two decades of the century. Even if we do not go back so far, even if we only speak of the recent past — whose memory, whose shadow even, still reaches over us today — no one can deny that for thirty years we lived through a period of ordeals,

---

1. A few examples, remaining at the *theoretical* level: the economist evolutionism of Stalin's *Dialectical Materialism and Historical Materialism*; the conjuring away of the historical role of Trotsky and others in the Bolshevik Revolution (*Short History of the CPSU [B]*); the thesis of the sharpening of the class struggle under socialism; the formula: 'everything depends on the cadres', etc. Among ourselves: the thesis of 'bourgeois science/proletarian science', the thesis of 'absolute pauperization', etc.

heroism and dramas under the domination of a political line and political practices which, for lack of a concept, we have to call by a proper name: that of Stalin. Do we quite simply leave all this behind as a consequence of Stalin's death and on the strength (and through the effects) of a little phrase: 'the personality cult,' pronounced at the Twentieth Congress of the Communist Party of the Soviet Union as the 'last word' (in every possible sense) in the affair? I wrote, during the 1960s, in a philosophical text which John Lewis has right in front of him, that the concept of the 'personality cult' was a concept which '*cannot be found* in *Marxist theory*', that it had no value in terms of knowledge, that it explained nothing and left us in the dark. This was quite clear: it still is.

'A concept which cannot be found in Marxist *theory*.' This must be recognized. In the form in which it was put forward and used, both theoretically and politically, the concept of the 'personality cult' was not simply the name of something: it did not satisfy itself with simply pointing out the *facts* (the 'abuses', the 'violations of Soviet legality'). It claimed at the same time – this was openly stated – *theoretical* pretensions: it was supposed to give an account of the 'essence' of the facts which it revealed. And this is how it was used politically.

Now this pseudo-concept, the circumstances of whose solemn and dramatic pronouncements are well known, did indeed expose certain practices: 'abuses', 'errors', and in certain cases 'crimes'. But it explained nothing of their conditions, of their causes, in short of their *internal* determination, and therefore of their forms.[2] Yet since it *claimed* to explain

2. For Marxism the explanation of any phenomenon is in the last instance *internal*: it is the *internal* 'contradiction' which is the 'motor'. The external circumstances are active: but 'through' the internal contradiction which they overdetermine. Why the need to be precise on this question? Because certain Communists, finding the 'explanation' in terms of the 'cult' inadequate, thought of

what in fact it did not explain, this pseudo-concept could only mislead those whom it was supposed to instruct. Must we be even more explicit? To reduce the grave events of thirty years of Soviet and Communist history to this pseudo-explanation by the 'cult' was not and could not have been a simple mistake, an oversight of an intellectual hostile to the practice of divine worship: it was, as we all know, a political act of responsible leaders, a certain *one-sided* way of putting forward the problems, not of what is vulgarly called 'Stalin-ism', but of what must, I think, be called (unless one objects to *thinking* about it) by the name of a concept: provisionally, the *'Stalinian' deviation*.[3] And, at the same time, it was a certain way of *not posing* the problems. More precisely, it was (and still is) a way of seeking the causes of grave events and of their forms in certain defects of the functioning of the *legal* superstructure ('violations of socialist legality'), without

the idea of adding a *supplement*, which could only be *external*: for example, the explanation by capitalist encirclement, whose reality no one can deny. Marxism, however, does not like supplements: when you need a supplement too much, you have probably missed the *internal* cause.

3. The term 'Stalinism', which the Soviet leaders have avoided using, but which was widely used by bourgeois ideologians and the Trotskyists, before penetrating into Communist circles, offers in general the same 'disadvantages' as the term 'personality cult'. It designates a *reality* which innumerable Communists, above all, have experienced, either in direct and tragic form, or less directly and with more or less serious consequences. Now this terminology also has theoretical pretensions: among bourgeois ideologists and many Trotskyists. It *explains* nothing. To set out on the road of a Marxist explanation, to be able to pose the problem of the explanation of these facts, the least that is required is to put forward *Marxist concepts*, and to see whether they are suitable. That is why I am proposing the concept of '*deviation*', which is a concept that can certainly be 'found' in Marxist-Leninist theory. Thus one might, first of all, talk of a '*Stalin-ian' deviation*: first of all, because to talk of a deviation necessarily requires that it should next be *qualified*, that one should explain *in what* it consisted, and always in Marxist terms. One thing, at the present stage, must be made clear: to speak of a 'Stalinian' deviation is not to explain it by an individual, who would be its 'cause'. The adjective certainly refers to a man in history, but above all to a cer-tain *period* in the history of the International Labour Movement.

(even in the form of a hypothesis!) looking into the whole of the State Apparatuses constituting the Superstructure (the Repressive Apparatus, the Ideological Apparatuses, including the Party), and above all without getting to the root of the problem (one which was so serious and lasted so long): the *contradictions* of the construction of socialism and of its line, that is, without dealing with the existing forms of production relations, class relations and the class struggle, the last of which is then said – in a formula which has not yet been withdrawn – to have been 'transcended' in the USSR. Yet this is where the *internal* causes of the facts of the 'cult' must be sought – at the risk of finding other facts.

Of course, it is not true that everything is always connected with everything else – this is not a Marxist thesis – and one does not need to invoke the whole infrastructure and superstructure to sort out a simple legal detail, if it is only a *detail*, and only *legal*. But is the 'Stalin' deviation a detail? A simple legal detail?! Of course, one cannot, at any and every moment, in a moment, remake what many years have unmade – this is not a Marxist thesis. There are of course historical constructions which are so interconnected with neighbouring buildings, which are so much propped up by these latter that one cannot simply and brutally chop down their surroundings to give them some air: one must sometimes proceed 'cautiously'. But the precautions of the Twentieth Congress . . . !

The 'Stalinian' deviation, in the form revealed to us by the terms of the official declarations, pointed out certain facts, without – for lack of Marxist explanations – avoiding the trap of repeating much earlier denunciations: those of the most anti-Communist bourgeois ideology, and those of the 'anti-Stalinist' theory of Trotskyism. *As it was revealed to us*, limited in its scope to 'violations of socialist *legality*' alone – while the Communists of the USSR and of the world had an infinitely more 'extensive' experience of it – this deviation could, finally, only provoke two possible reactions (leaving aside its 'classical' exploitation by anti-Communist and anti-Soviet elements). *Either a left-wing critique*, which accepts the term 'deviation', even if in a very contradictory sense, and which, in order, to *account for it*, undertakes serious research into its basic historical causes: that is, if John Lewis will excuse me, not into Man (or Personality), but into the Superstructure, relations of production, and therefore the state of class relations and the class struggle in the USSR. Such a critique may then, but only then, be justified in talking not only about a violation of the law but also about the reasons for this violation. *Or a right-wing critique*, which attacks only certain aspects of the *legal* superstructure, and of course can then invoke Man and his Rights, and oppose Man to the violation of his Rights (or simple 'workers' councils' to the 'bureaucracy').

The fact is: one practically *never* hears anything but the second critique. And the official formulation of the critique of the 'cult', of the 'violations of socialist legality', far from keeping the most violent bourgeois anti-Communism and Trotskyist anti-Stalinism at arm's length, actually provides them with a historical argument *they could hardly have hoped for*: it gives them a justification, a second wind, a second life. Which explains, let it be said in passing, a good number of apparently paradoxical phenomena: for example, the resurgence fifty years after the October Revolution and twenty years after the Chinese Revolution of Organizations which have lasted forty years *without winning a single historical victory* (because, unlike some of the present-day 'ultra-left', they are organizations, and they also have a theory): the Trotskyist Organizations. And that is not to speak of the 'effectiveness' of bourgeois anti-Sovietism, thirty years after Stalingrad!

However that may be, we did not need to wait long

before seeing the official critique of the 'Stalinian' deviation, that of the 'personality cult', produce – in the special circumstances – its inevitable ideological effects. After the Twentieth Congress an openly rightist wave carried off (to speak only of them) many Marxist and Communist 'intellectuals', not only in the capitalist countries, but also in the socialist countries. It is not of course a question of putting the intellectuals of the socialist countries and Western Marxists into the same bag – and especially not of confusing the mass political protest of our comrades in Prague, known as 'socialism with a human face', with Garaudy's 'integral humanism', etc. In Prague they did not have the same choice of words (the words did not have the same sense) nor the same choice of roads. But here . . . ! Here we see Communists following the Social-Democrats and even religious thinkers (who used to have an almost guaranteed monopoly in these things) in the practice of *exploiting* the works of Marx's youth in order to draw out of them an ideology of Man, Liberty, Alienation, Transcendence, etc. – without asking whether the *system* of these notions with idealist or materialist, whether this ideology was petty-bourgeois or proletarian. 'Orthodoxy', as John Lewis says, was almost submerged: not Stalin's 'thought', which continued and continues to hold itself comfortably above the uproar, in its bases, its 'line' and certain of its practices – but quite simply the theory of Marx and Lenin.

It was in these conditions that I came to intervene, let us say 'accidentally', in the form of a critical review I wrote of a number of Soviet and East German articles which had been translated into French. This review, 'On the Young Marx', appeared in the magazine *La Pensée* in 1960.* I was trying to the best of my ability and with the makeshift tools at my disposal, by criticizing a few received ideas and asking a few

---

* Reprinted in *For Marx* [Translator's note]

questions, to combat the contagion which was 'menacing' us. That is how it was. At the beginning there were not very many of us, and John Lewis is right: 'we' were crying 'in the wilderness'. But one must be very wary of this kind of 'wilderness'; or rather, know how not to be frightened by it. In reality 'we' have never been alone. Communists are never alone.

So, against the rightist-idealist interpretations of Marxist theory as a 'philosophy of man', of Marxism as a theoretical humanism; against the tendentious confusion – whether positivist or subjectivist – of science and Marxist 'philosophy; against the evolutionist reduction of the materialist dialectic to the 'Hegelian' dialectic; and in general against bourgeois and petty-bourgeois positions, I have tried to defend, we have tried to defend, come what may, at the cost of rash actions and errors, a few vital ideas which can be summed up in a single idea: that which is special and specific to Marx, which is revolutionary in both the theoretical and political senses, and this in the face of bourgeois and petty-bourgeois ideology, with which he had to *break* in order to become a Communist and found the science of history, the same ideology with which even today we must still and always will have to *break*, to become, remain or become again Marxists.

The forms may have changed: but the root of the question has remained, for 150 years or so, substantially the same. This bourgeois ideology, which is the *dominant* ideology, and which weighs so heavily on the labour movement and threatens its most vital functions – unless the movement fights resolutely back on the basis of its *own positions*, quite exterior to bourgeois ideology because *proletarian* – this bourgeois ideology is actually, in its deepest essence, constituted by the ideological pair *economism/humanism*. Behind the abstract categories of the philosophy which provides it with titles and airs, it was this pair of notions which I was aiming at when I made a joint attack, *both* on theoretical humanism (I repeat: theoretical; not on a word, or a few phrases, or even an inspired idea of the future, but on a *philosophical* language in which 'man' is a category with a *theoretical function*) *and*, passing by the vulgar forms of Hegelianism or evolutionism which join with it, on *economism*.

For no one (at least, no revolutionary Marxist) can fail to see that when, in the midst of the class struggle, the litanies of humanism hold the theoretical and ideological stage, it is economism which is quietly winning. Even under feudalism, when humanist ideology was revolutionary, it was still profoundly bourgeois. In a bourgeois class society it always has played and still does play the role of hiding the class-determined economic and economistic practices governed by the relations of production, exploitation and exchange, and by bourgeois law. In a bourgeois class society there is always the risk that humanist ideology – when it is not just a slip of the pen or an image of political rhetoric, when it is of a lasting and organic character – serves as a cover for an *economistic* deviation in the workers' organizations, which are not immune to the contagion of the dominant ideology. This deviation is in principled contradiction to proletarian class positions. The whole history of the Rights of Man proves it: behind Man, it is Bentham who comes out the victor.[4] Much of the history of the Second International, whose dominant tendency Lenin denounced, also goes to prove it: behind Bernstein's neo-Kantian idealism, it is the economist current which comes out on top. Who can seriously claim that the whole of this long history, with all its conflicts and dangers, is behind us, and that it will never again menace us, that we shall never again be at risk?

4. Karl Marx, *Capital*, vol. 1, Part I, section 2.

I am talking about the ideological *pair* economism/humanism. It is a pair in which the two terms are complementary. It is not an accidental link, but an organic and consubstantial one. It is born spontaneously, that is to say necessarily, of the bourgeois practices of production and exploitation, *and at the same time* of the legal practices of bourgeois law and its ideology, which provide a sanction for the capitalist relations of production and exploitation and their reproduction.

And it is quite true that bourgeois ideology is fundamentally *economist*, that the capitalist sees everything from the point of view of commodity relations and from the point of view of the material conditions (means of production are also commodities) which allow him to exploit that very special 'commodity', the labour power of the workers. Thus, he sees things from the point of view of the *techniques* of the extortion of surplus-value (which are linked together with capitalist organization and division of labour), from the point of view of the technology of exploitation, of economic 'performance' and development: from the point of view of capitalist accumulation. And what does the Bourgeois Economist do? Marx showed that, even when he raised himself to the point of thinking in terms of capitalism, he did no more than theorize the economistic viewpoint of the capitalist. Marx criticized the very project of 'Political Economy', *as such, because it was economistic*.

But at the same time it is true that the reverse side of the same coin, the necessary 'cover', the alibi, the 'point of honour' of this economism is humanism or bourgeois liberalism. This is because ideas find their foundations in the categories of Bourgeois *Law* and the legal ideology materially indispensable to the functioning of Bourgeois Law: liberty of the Person, that is, in principle, his right freely to dispose of himself, his right to his property, his free will and his body (the proletarian: a Person 'free' to sell himself!), and his other goods (private property: real property – which abolishes others – that of the means of production).

This is the breeding ground of economism/humanism: the capitalist mode of production and exploitation. And this is the precise link by which, the precise place in which these two ideologies join together as a *pair: Bourgeois Law*, which at the same time both provides a real support for capitalist relations of production, and lends its categories to liberal and humanist ideology, including bourgeois philosophy.

The question then arises: when this bourgeois ideological pair penetrates into Marxism, 'when it pursues the struggle, not on its own terrain but on the general terrain of Marxism, as revisionism' (Lenin), what does it become? It remains what it was before: a *bourgeois* point of view, but this time 'functioning' within Marxism. As astonishing as this may seem, the whole history of the Labour Movement and Lenin's theses are witness to it:[5] Marxism itself can, in certain circumstances, be considered and treated as, *even practiced as a bourgeois point of view*. Not only by 'armchair Marxists', who reduce it to academic bourgeois sociology, and who are never anything but 'functionaries of the dominant ideology' – but also by sections of the Labour Movement, and their leaders.

This is something which depends on the relations of power in the class struggle, and, at the same time, on *class position* in the class struggle, in the 'line', the organization and the functioning of the class struggle fought by the Labour Movement. That is to say that it is a historical form in which the *fusion* between the Labour Movement and Marxist theory – which alone can assure the *objectively* 'revolutionary' character of the 'movement' (Lenin) – is held up

5. Cf. *Marxism and Revisionism, The Collapse of the Second International*, The Renegade Kautsky, etc.

or reversed, in the face of what must perhaps, for purposes of understanding, also be called a 'fusion': but quite another kind of 'fusion', that between the Labour Movement and bourgeois ideology.

The economism/humanism pair, when it is introduced into Marxism, does not really change in form, even if it is forced to make some changes (only some) in its vocabulary. Humanism remains humanism: it takes on a Social-Democratic accent, one which raises not the question of the *class struggle* and its abolition, through the emancipation of the *working class*, but that of the defence of Human Rights, of liberty and justice, even of the liberation and free development of the 'personality' or the 'integral personality'. Economism remains economism: for example, in the exaltation of the development of the Productive Forces, of their 'socialization' (what kind of socialization?), of the 'scientific and technical revolution', of 'productivity', etc.

Can we make a comparison? Yes, we can. And we discover the factor which permits us to identify the ideological pair *economism/humanism* and its practices as bourgeois: it is the elimination of something which never figures in economism or humanism, *the elimination of the relations of production and of the class struggle*.

The fact that the bourgeoisie, in its own ideology, keeps *silent* about the relations of production and the class struggle, in order to exalt not only 'expansion' and 'productivity' but also Man and his liberty — that is its own affair, and it is quite in order, in *bourgeois order*: because it needs this silence, which allows economism/humanism, expressing *the bourgeois point of view*, to work at the concealment of the relations of production while helping to guarantee and reproduce them. But when the Workers' Parties, before the revolution, or even after, themselves keep *silent* (or semi-silent) about the relations of production, the class struggle, and their concrete forms,[6] while exalting *both* the Productive Forces *and* Man – this is quite a different matter! Because unless it is only a question of words or of a few speeches, if it is really a question of a consistent political line and practice, then you can bet – as Lenin did, when he spoke about the pre-1914 Second International – that this bourgeois point of view is a contaminating agent which can threaten or even overcome the *proletarian point of view* within *Marxism itself*.

And since we have been talking about the Second International, let us say a brief word about the Third, about the last ten years of its existence. After all, why be silent about a question which is burning to be expressed? Why meet the official silence with nothing but another silence, and thus give it sanction? For an official silence does still reign – beneath a facade of feigned or embarrassed 'explanations' – over this period, one whose heroism, whose greatness, whose dramas we have lived through or known. Why should we not try to *understand*, whatever the risks of what we say, not only the merits of the International but also the inevitable *contradictions* of its positions and its line (and how could it have avoided them, especially given the tragic times with which it had to deal)? I am rather afraid that we may one day have to recognize the existence within it of a certain *tendency* which, held in bounds by Lenin's efforts, could not finally be mastered, and ended up by quietly taking over the leading role. I am rather afraid that a long time might be allowed to go by – for apparently pragmatic reasons, which doubtless have deeper roots – before a 'hypothesis' such as that which I want to put forward today could hope to be stated in black and white, and *put to the test of a genuine Marxist analysis*. I shall take the personal risk of advancing this

---

6. Lenin: in the 'transition' between capitalism and communism, classes remain, the class struggle remains, but *takes on new forms*.

hypothesis now, in the form of necessarily schematic propositions:

1. The International Communist Movement has been affected since the 1930s, to different degrees and in very different ways in different countries and organizations, by the effects of a *single* deviation, which can provisionally be called the 'Stalinian deviation'.

2. Keeping things *well in proportion*, that is to say, respecting essential distinctions, but nevertheless going beyond the most obvious phenomena – which are, in spite of their extremely serious character, historically secondary: I mean those which are generally grouped together in Communist Parties under the heading 'personality cult' and 'dogmatism' – the Stalinian deviation can be considered as *a form* (a *special form*, converted by the state of the world class struggle, the existence of a single socialist State, and the State power held by the Bolshevik Party) of the *posthumous revenge of the Second International*: as a revival of its main tendency.

3. This main tendency was, as we know, basically an economistic one.

This is only a hypothesis, and I am simply laying down its reference points. It naturally poses very great problems. The most obvious of these problems can be stated in the following way: *how* could a basically economistic tendency have combined with the superstructural effects we know so well, effects which it produced as the transformation of its own forms? *What* were the material forms of existence of this tendency, which enabled it to produce these effects in the existing conjuncture? *How* did this tendency, centred from a certain time onwards on the USSR, spread through the whole International Communist Movement, and what special – and sometimes differing – forms did it take?

If some readers are disconcerted by the comparison between the economism of the Second International and that of the 'Stalinian deviation', I will first of all reply: you must look and see what is the *first* principle of analysis recommended and used by Lenin at the beginning of Chapter 7 of *The Collapse of the Second International* to help understand a *deviation* in the history of the Labour Movement. The first thing you have to do is to see if this deviation is not 'linked *with some former current of socialism*'. Not because of some vulgar 'historicism', but because there exists a continuity, in the history of the Labour Movement, of its difficulties, its problems, its *contradictions*, of correct solutions and therefore *also of its deviations*, because of the continuity of a single class struggle against the bourgeoisie, and of a single class struggle (economic, political *and ideological-theoretical*) of the bourgeoisie against the Labour Movement. The possibility of cases of 'posthumous revenge', of 'revivals', is based on this continuity.

But I would like to add something else. There are of course serious political questions at stake in the summary and schematic hypotheses which I am proposing – but, above all, there exists the possibility of serious ambiguities which must at all costs be guarded against. Look how Lenin – who was uncompromising in his denunciation of the idealist-economist tendency of the Second International – treated this very organization: he never *reduced* the Second International to its deviation. He recognized the different periods in its history, he distinguished the main question from the secondary one – and, for example, he always gave the International credit for having developed the organizations of the proletarian class struggle, the trade unions and workers' parties; nor did he ever refuse to cite Kautsky, or to defend Plekhanov's philosophical work. In the same way, and for infinitely more obvious and powerful reasons, Stalin cannot be *reduced* to the deviation which we have linked to his name; even less can this be done with the Third International which he came in the thirties to dominate. He had other historical merits. He understood that it was *necessary* to abandon the miraculous idea of an imminent 'world revolution' and to undertake instead the 'construction of socialism' in one country. And he drew the consequences: it must be defended at any cost as the foundation and last line of defence of socialism throughout the world, it must be made into an impregnable fortress capable of withstanding the imperialist siege; and, to that end, it must be provided with a heavy industry. It was this very industry that turned out the Stalingrad tanks which served the heroic struggle of the Soviet people in their fight to the death to liberate the world from Nazism. Our history *also* passed in that direction. And in spite of the deformations, caricatures and tragedies for which this period is responsible, it must be recalled that millions of Communists also learned, even if Stalin 'taught' them in dogmatic form, that there existed *Principles of Leninism*.

Thus, if it seems possible, keeping everything *in proportion*, to talk about the posthumous revenge of the Second International, it must be added that it is a revenge which took place in other times, in other circumstances, and of course in other *forms*, which cannot be the subject of a literal comparison. But in spite of these considerable differences one can talk about the revenge, or the revival, or the resurgence of a tendency which is *basically* the same: of an economistic conception and 'line', even when these were hidden by declarations which were, in their own way, cruelly 'humanist' (the slogan 'Man, the most precious capital', the measures and dispositions, which remained a dead letter, of the Soviet Constitution of 1936).

If this is true, if the 'Stalinian' deviation cannot be reduced to 'violations of Soviet legality' alone; if it is related to more profound causes in history and in the *conception* of the class struggle and of class *position*; and even supposing that the Soviet people are now protected from all violations of *legality* – it does not follow that either they or we have completely overcome the 'Stalinian' deviation (neither the causes, nor the mechanisms, nor the effects of which have been the object of a 'concrete analysis' in the Leninist sense, that is to say, of a scientific Marxist analysis) *simply on account of the denunciation of the 'personality cult'*, or by a patient work of rectification unenlightened by any analysis. In these conditions, with all the information, past and present, available to us (including the official silence, which refuses to pronounce against these facts), we can bet that the Stalinian 'line', purged of 'violations of legality' and therefore 'liberalized' – with economism and humaninism working together – has, for better or worse, survived Stalin and – it should not be astonishing! – the Twentieth Congress. One is even justified in supposing that, behind the talk about the different varieties of 'humanism', whether restrained or not, this 'line' continues to pursue an honourable career, in a peculiar kind of silence, a sometimes talkative and sometimes mute silence, which is now and again broken by the noise of an explosion or a split.

So that I do not have to leave anything out of consideration, I will advance one more risky hypothesis which will certainly 'say something' to John Lewis, specialist of Chinese politics. If we look back over our whole history of the last forty years or more, it seems to me that, in reckoning up the account (which is not an easy thing to do), the only *historically existing* (left) 'critique' of the fundamentals of the 'Stalinian deviation' to be found – and which, moreover, is *contemporary* with this very deviation, and thus for the most part precedes the Twentieth Congress – is a concrete critique, one which exists in the facts, in the struggle, in the line, in the practices, their principles and their forms, of the Chinese Revolution. A silent critique, which speaks through its actions, the result of the political and ideological struggles of the Revolution, from the Long March to the Cultural Revolution and its results. A critique *from afar*. A critique 'from behind the scenes'. To be looked at more closely, to be interpreted. A *contradictory* critique, moreover – if only because of the disproportion between acts and texts. Whatever you like: but a critique from which one can learn, which can help us to test our hypotheses, that is, help us to see our own history more clearly. But here too, of course, we have to speak in terms of a tendency and of specific forms – without letting the forms mask the tendency and its contradictions.

If I have been able – with the means at my disposal, and from afar – even very feebly to echo these historic struggles and to indicate, behind their ideological effects, the existence of some real problems: this, for a Communist philosopher, is no more than his duty.

These, to go no further, are some of the very concrete 'questions' – where politics stares you in the face – which haunt the margins of the simple philosophical work undertaken by me, for better or worse, more than ten years ago.

As far as John Lewis is concerned, it seems that it never occurred to him to ask such questions! From our point of view I hope that it is so. Because the matter would be that much more serious if, having understood what was at stake, he had kept silent about it: so as not to get his fingers burned.

June 1972

Remark on the Category:
'Process without a Subject or Goal(s)'

This formula ['process without a Subject', 'process without a Subject or Goal(s)'] has everything required to offend against the 'evidence' of common sense, that is (Gramsci) of the dominant ideology, and thus without any trouble at all to make some determined enemies.

For example, the objection will be raised that 'the masses' and 'classes' are, when all is said and done, 'made up of' *men*! And that, if Man (a category which is then simply declared to be . . . an 'abstraction', or, to add weight, a 'speculative abstraction') cannot be said to make history, at least *men* do so – concrete, living men, human subjects. In support of this idea Marx himself will be cited as witness, his testimony being the *beginning* of a little remark in the *Eighteenth Brumaire*: 'Men make their own history . . . ' With the backing of evidence and quote, the conclusion is quickly drawn: history has 'subjects'; these subjects are obviously 'men'; 'men' are therefore, if not the Subject of history, at least *the subjects* of history . . .

This kind of reasoning unfortunately only stands up at the cost of confusions, sliding meanings and ideological word-games: on Man-men, Subject-subjects, etc.

Let us be careful, therefore, not to play with words, and let us look at the thing a bit closer.

In my opinion: men (plural), in the concrete sense, are

necessarily subjects (plural) *in* history, because they act *in* history as subjects (plural). But there is no Subject (singular) *of* history. And I will go even further: 'men' are not 'the subjects' *of* history. Let me explain.

To understand these distinctions one must define the *nature* of the question at issue. The question of the constitution of individuals as historical *subjects*, active *in* history, has nothing in principle to do with the question of *the 'Subject of* history', or even with that of *the 'subjects of* history'. The first question is of a *scientific* kind: it concerns historical materialism. The second question is of a *philosophical* kind: it concerns dialectical materialism.

First question: *scientific*.

That human, i.e. social individuals are *active* in history – as *agents* of the different social practices of the historical process of production and reproduction – that is a fact. But, considered as *agents*, human individuals are not 'free' and 'constitutive' subjects in the philosophical sense of these terms. They work in and through the determinations of the *forms of historical existence* of the social relations of production and reproduction (labour process, division and organization of labour, process of production and reproduction, class struggle, etc.). But that is not all. These agents can only be agents *if they are subjects*. This I think I showed in my article on 'Ideology and Ideological State Apparatuses'. [See *Lenin and Philosophy and other Essays*, London NLB, 1971] No human, i.e. social individual can be the agent of a practice if he does not have the *form of a subject*. The 'subject-form' is actually the form of historical existence of every individual, of every agent of social practices: because the social relations of production and reproduction necessarily comprise, as an *integral part*, what Lenin calls '(juridico-) *ideological social relations*', which, in order to function, impose the subject-form on each agent-individual. The agent-individuals thus always act in the subject-form, as subjects. But the fact that they are necessarily subjects does not make the agents of social-historical practices into the *subject* or *subjects* of history (in the philosophical sense of the term: *subject of*). The subject-agents are only active *in* history through the determination of the relations of production and reproduction, and in their forms.

Second question: *philosophical*.

It is for precise ideological ends that bourgeois philosophy has taken the legal-ideological notion of the *subject*, made it into a philosophical category, its number one philosophical category, and posed the question of *the* Subject of knowledge (the *ego* of the cogito, the Kantian or Husserlian transcendental subject, etc.), of morality, etc., and of *the Subject of* history. This illusory question does of course have a purpose, but in its position and form it has *no sense* as far as dialectical materialism is concerned, which purely and simply rejects it, as it rejects (for example) the question of God's existence. In advancing the Thesis of a 'process without a Subject or Goal(s)', I want simply but clearly to say this. To be dialectical-materialist, Marxist philosophy must break with the idealist category of the 'Subject' as Origin, Essence and Cause, *responsible* in its internality for all the determinations of the external 'Object',[1] of which it is said to be the internal 'Subject'. For Marxist philosophy there can be no Subject as an Absolute Centre, as a Radical Origin, as a Unique Cause. Nor can one, in order to get out of the problem, rely on a category like that of the 'ex-Centration of the Essence' (Lucien Sève), since it is an illusory compromise which – using a fraudulently 'radical' term, one whose root is perfectly conformist (*ex-centration*) – safeguards the

1. The category of 'process without a Subject or Goal(s)' **can therefore take the** form: '*process without a Subject or Object*'.

umbilical cord between Essence and Centre and therefore
remains a prisoner of idealist philosophy: since there is no
Centre, every *ex*-centration is superfluous or a sham. In
reality Marxist philosophy thinks in and according to quite
different categories: determination in the last instance –
which is quite different from the Origin, Essence or Cause
unes – determination by Relations (*idem*), contradiction,
process, 'nodal points' (Lenin), etc.: in short, in quite a different configuration and according to quite different categories from classical idealist philosophy.

Naturally, these philosophical categories do not only concern history.

But if we *restrict* ourselves to history (which is what concerns us here), the philosophical question presents itself in
the following terms. There is no question of contesting the
gains of historical materialism, which says that individuals
are agent-subjects *in* history under the determination of the
forms of existence of the relations of production and reproduction. It is a question of something quite different: of
knowing whether history can be thought philosophically, in
its modes of determination, according to the idealist category of the *Subject*. The position of dialectical materialism on
this question seems quite clear to me. One cannot seize
(*begreifen*: conceive), that is to say, *think* real history (the
process of the reproduction of social formations and their
revolutionary transformation) as if it could be reduced to *an*
Origin, *an* Essence, or *a* Cause (even Man), which would be
its Subject – a Subject, a 'being' or 'essence', held to be *identifiable*, that is to say existing in the form of the *unity* of an
internality, and (theoretically and practically *responsible*
identity, internality and responsibility are constitutive,
among other things, of every subject), thus accountable,
thus capable of *accounting for* the whole of the 'phenomena'
of history.

The matter is quite clear when we are confronted with classical idealism, which, within the openly stated category of liberty, takes Man (= the Human Race = Humanity) to be the Subject and the Goal of history; cf the *Enlightenment*, and Kant, the 'purest' philosopher of bourgeois ideology. The matter is also clear when we are confronted with the *philosophical* petty-bourgeois communitarian *anthropology* of Feuerbach (still respected by Marx in the 1844 Manuscripts), in which the Essence of Man is the Origin, Cause and Goal of history.

But the same position evidently takes on a more deceptive air in the post-Husserlian and pre-Kantian (Cartesian) phenomenological interpretations, like those of Sartre, where the Kantian Theses of the Transcendental *Subject*, unique because one, and of the Liberty of *Humanity*, are mixed up and 'squashed together', and where the Subject is multiplied within a theory of the *originating* Liberty of an infinity of 'concrete' transcendental subjects (Tran Duc Thao said, explaining Husserl: 'We are all, you and I, each one of us, 'transcendental egos' and 'transcendental equals' ["*egos*" and "*egaux*"]', which brings us back to the Thesis that 'men' (the concrete individuals) are *the* subjects (transcendental, constitutive) of history). This is the basis of Sartre's special interest in a 'little phrase' from the *Eighteenth Brumaire*, and a similar phrase from Engels, which fit him like a glove. Now this position – which brings the Kantian categories *down* to the level, no longer of an anthropological philosophy (Feuerbach), but of a vulgar philosophical psychosociology – not only has nothing to do with Marxism, but actually constitutes a quite dubious theoretical position which it is practically impossible to *conceive* and to defend. You just have to read the *Critique of Dialectical Reason*, which announces an Ethics that never appeared, to be convinced of this point.

In proposing the category of the 'process without a Subject or Goal(s)', we thus draw a 'demarcation line' (Lenin) between dialectical-materialist positions and bourgeois or petty-bourgeois idealist positions. Naturally, one cannot expect *everything* from a first intervention. This 'demarcation line' must be 'worked on'. But, as Lenin said for his part, a demarcation line – if it is correct – is in principle sufficient, just as it is, to defend us from idealism and to mark out the way forward.

These philosophical positions are of course not without their consequences. Not only, for example, do they imply that Marxism has nothing to do with the 'anthropological question' ('What is man?'), or with a theory of the realization-objectification-alienation-disalienation of the *Human Essence* (as in Feuerbach and his heirs: theoreticians of *philosophical* reification and fetishism), or even with the theory of the 'excentration of the Human Essence', which only criticizes the idealism of the Subject from within the limits of the idealism of the Subject, dressed up with the attributes of the 'ensemble of social relations' of the sixth *Thesis on Feuerbach* – but they also allow us to understand the sense of Marx's famous 'little phrase' in the *Eighteenth Brumaire*.

This comment, in its *complete* form, reads as follows: 'Men make their own history, but they do not make it out of freely chosen elements (*aus freien Stücken*), under circumstances chosen by themselves, but under circumstances (*Umstände*) directly encountered (*vorgefundene*), given by and transmitted from the past.' And – as if he had foreseen the exploitation of these first five words, and even these 'circumstances' from which Sartre draws out such dazzling effects of the 'practico-inert', that is, of liberty – Marx, in the Preface to the *Eighteenth Brumaire*, written seventeen years later (in 1869, two years after *Capital*), set down the following lines: 'I show something quite different (*different* from the ideology of Hugo and of Proudhon, who both hold the individual Napoleon III to be the [detestable or glorious] *cause 'responsible'* for the *coup d'état*), namely how the *class struggle* (Marx's emphasis) in France created the circumstances (*Umstände*) and the relations (*Verhältnisse*) which allowed (*ermöglicht*) a person (a subject) so mediocre and grotesque to play the role of a hero'.

One must read one's authors closely. History really is a 'process without a Subject or Goal(s)', where the given *circumstances* in which 'men' act as subjects under the determination of social *relations* are the product of the *class struggle*. History therefore does not have a Subject, in the philosophical sense of the term, but a *motor*: that very class struggle.

1 May 1973

PUBLISHER'S NOTE TO 'FREUD AND LACAN'

Louis Althusser agreed to let New Left Review *reproduce the following article, which was written in 1964 and published in the French Communist Party journal,* La Nouvelle Critique.

In a letter to the translator (21 February 1969), Louis Althusser wrote: 'There is a danger that this text will be misunderstood, unless it is taken for what it then objectively was: a philosophical intervention urging members of the PCF to recognize the scientificity of psycho-analysis, of Freud's work, and the importance of Lacan's interpretation of it. Hence it was polemical, for psycho-analysis had been officially condemned in the fifties as "a reactionary ideology", and, despite some modification, this condemnation still dominated the situation when I wrote this article. This exceptional situation must be taken into account when the meaning of my interpretation is assessed today.'

Louis Althusser also warned English readers that his article contained theses that must 'either *be corrected, or* expanded'.

'In particular, in the article Lacan's theory is presented in terms which, despite all precautions, have "culturalist" *overtones (whereas Lacan's theory is profoundly* anti-culturalist).

'On the other hand, the suggestions at the end of the article are correct and deserve a much extended treatment, that is, the

*discussion of the forms of familial ideology, and of the crucial
role they play in initiating the functioning of the instance that
Freud called "the unconscious", but which should be re-
christened as soon as a better term is found.*

   '*This mention of the forms of familial ideology (the ideology
of paternity-maternity-conjugality-infancy and their inter-
actions) is crucial, for it implies the following conclusion –
that Lacan could not express, given his theoretical formation –
that is, that* no theory of psycho-analysis can be produced
without basing it on historical materialism (*on which the
theory of the formations of familial ideology depends, in the
last instance*).'

AUTHOR'S PREFATORY NOTE

Let us admit, without prevarication: anyone today who
merely wants to understand Freud's revolutionary discovery, who wants to know what it means as well as just
recognizing its existence, has to make a great theoretical and
critical effort in order to cross the vast space of ideological
prejudice that divides us from Freud. For not only has
Freud's discovery been reduced, as we shall see, to disciplines
which are essentially foreign to it (biology, psychology,
sociology, philosophy); not only have many psycho-analysts
(notably in the American school) becomes accomplices to
this revisionism; but, more important, this revisionism has
itself objectively assisted the fantastic ideological exploitation whose object and victim psycho-analysis has been.
Not without good reason did French Marxists once (in
1948) denounce this exploitation as a 'reactionary ideology'
which furnished arguments for the ideological struggle
against Marxism, and a practical instrument for the intimi-
dation and mystification of consciousnesses.

But today it must also be said that, in their own way, these same Marxists were directly or indirectly the first victims of the ideology they denounced; for they confused this ideology and Freud's revolutionary discovery, thereby adopting in practice the enemy's position, accepting his conditions and recognizing the image he had imposed on them as the supposed reality of psycho-analysis. The whole history of the relations between Marxism and psycho-analysis depends essentially on this confusion, this imposture.

That this was particularly difficult to avoid we can understand from the function of this ideology: the 'dominant' ideas, in this case, were playing their 'dominating' role to perfection, ruling unrecognized over the very minds that were trying to fight them. But it is explained by the existence of the pyscho-analytic revisionism that made this exploitation possible: the fall into ideology began in fact with the fall of psycho-analysis into biologism, psychologism and sociologism.

We can also see that this revisionism could derive its authority from the ambiguity of some of Freud's concepts, for, like all inventors, Freud was forced to think his discovery in existing theoretical concepts, i.e. concepts designed for other purposes (was not Marx, too, forced to think his discovery in certain Hegelian concepts?). This will come as no surprise to anyone at all familiar with the history of new sciences – and at all careful to discern the irreducible element of a discovery and of its objects in the concepts in which it was expressed at its birth, but which, out-dated by the advance of knowledge, may later mask it.

So a return to Freud today demands:

1. Not only that we reject the ideological layers of the reactionary exploitation of Freud as a crude mystification;

2. but also that we avoid the more subtle ambiguities of

psycho-analytic revisionism, sustained as they are by the prestige of certain more or less scientific disciplines;

3. and finally that we commit ourselves to a serious effort of historico-theoretical criticism in order to identify and define, in the concepts Freud had to use, the true *epistemological relation* between these concepts and their thought content.

Without this triple labour of ideological criticism (1,2) and epistemological elucidation (3), which, in France, has been initiated in practice by Lacan, Freud's discovery in its specificity will remain beyond our reach. And, more serious, we will take as Freud precisely what has been put within our reach, precisely what we aimed to reject (the reactionary ideological exploitation of Freud), or subscribed to more or less thoughtlessly (the different forms of bio-psycho-sociological revisionism). In either case, we would remain prisoners, at different levels, of the explicit or implicit categories of ideological exploitation and theoretical revisionism. Marxists, who know from their own experience the deformations Marx's enemies have imposed on his thought, can see why Freud could suffer the same fate, in his own way, and why an authentic 'return to Freud' is of such theoretical importance.

They will concede that if such a short article proposes to introduce a problem of this importance without betraying it, it must confine itself to the essential, it must situate the *object* of psycho-analysis so as to give a first definition of it, in concepts that allow its *location*, the indispensable precondition for its elucidation. They will concede therefore that, as far as possible, these concepts should be introduced in a rigorous form, as in any scientific discipline; to vulgarize them in an over-approximate commentary would banalize them, while an analysis that really drew them out would require much more space.

An accurate assessment of these concepts can only come from the serious study of Freud and Lacan which each one of us can undertake; the same is true for the definition of the still unsolved problems of this theoretical discipline already rich in results and promises.

Freud and Lacan

Friends have correctly criticized me for discussing Lacan in three lines.[1] This was too much for what I was saying about him, and too little for the conclusions that I drew from him. They have asked me for a few words to justify both the allusion and its object. Here they are – a few words, where a book is needed.

In the history of Western Reason, every care, foresight, precaution and warning has been devoted to births. Prenatal therapy is institutional. When a young science is born, the family circle is always ready for astonishment, jubilation and baptism. For a long time, every child, even the foundling, has been reputed the son of a father, and when it is a prodigy, the fathers would fight at the gate if it were not for the mother and the respect due to her. In our crowded world, a place is allocated for birth, a place is even allocated for the prediction of a birth: 'prospective'.

1. *Revue de l'Enseignement philosophique*, June–July 1963, 'Philosophie et sciences humaines', p. 7 and p. 11, n.14: 'Marx based his theory on the rejection of the myth of the *"homo œconomicus"*, Freud based his theory on the rejection of the myth of the *"homo psychologicus"*. Lacan has seen and understood Freud's liberating rupture. He has understood it in the fullest sense of the term, taking it rigorously at its word and forcing it to produce its own consequences, without concessions or quarter. It may be that, like everyone else, he errs in the detail or even the choice of his philosophical bearings; but we owe him the *essential*.'

To my knowledge, the nineteenth century saw the birth of two or three children that were not expected: Marx, Nietzsche and Freud. 'Natural' children, in the sense that nature offends customs, principles, morality and good breeding: nature is the rule violated, the unmarried mother, hence the absence of a legal father. Western Reason makes a fatherless child pay heavily. Marx, Nietzsche and Freud had to foot the often terrible bill of survival: a price compounded of exclusion, condemnation, insult, poverty, hunger and death, or madness. I speak only of them (other unfortunates might be mentioned who lived their death sentences in colour, sound and poetry). I speak only of them because they were the births of sciences or of criticism.

That Freud knew poverty, calumny and persecution, that his spirit was well enough anchored to withstand, and interpret, all the insults of the age – these things may have something to do with certain of the limits and dead-ends of his genius. An examination of this point is probably premature. Let us instead consider Freud's solitude in his own times. I do not mean human solitude (he had teachers and friends, though he went hungry), I mean *theoretical* solitude. For when he wanted to think i.e. to express in the form of a rigorous system of abstract concepts the extraordinary discovery that met him every day in his *practice*, search as he might for theoretical precedents, fathers in theory, he could find none. He had to cope with the following situation: to be himself his own father, to construct with his own craftsman's hands the theoretical space in which to situate his discovery, to weave with thread borrowed intuitively left and right the great net with which to catch in the depths of blind experience the teeming fish of the unconscious, which men call dumb because it speaks even while they sleep.

To express this in Kantian terms: Freud had to think his

discovery and his practice in *imported* concepts, concepts borrowed from the thermodynamic physics then dominant, from the political economy and biology of his time. With no legal inheritance behind him – except for a parcel of philosophical concepts (consciousness, preconsciousness, unconsciousness, etc.) which were probably more of a hindrance than a help as they were marked by a problematic of consciousness present even in its reservations – without any ancestral endowment whatever, his only forerunners writers – Sophocles, Shakespeare, Molière, Goethe – or proverbs, etc. Theoretically, Freud set up in business alone: producing his own 'home-made' concepts under the protection of imported concepts borrowed from the sciences as they existed, and, it should be said, from within the horizons of the ideological world in which these concepts swam.

That is how Freud comes to us. A long series of profound texts, sometimes clear, sometimes obscure, often enigmatic and contradictory, problematic, and armed with concepts many of which seem to us at first sight to be out of date, inadequate for their content, or surpassed. For today we cannot doubt the existence of this content: analytic practice itself, its effect.

So let us summarize the object Freud is for us:

1. A practice (the analytic cure). 2. A technique (the method of the cure) that gives rise to an abstract exposition with the appearance of a theory. 3. A theory which has a relation with the practice and the technique. This organic practical (1), technical (2) and theoretical (3) whole recalls the structure of every scientific discipline. *Formally*, what Freud gives us does have the structure of a science. Formally; for the difficulties of Freud's conceptual terminology, the sometimes material disproportion between his concepts and their content, suggest the question: in this organic

practico-technico-theoretical whole do we have a whole that is truly stabilized and founded at the scientific level? In other words, is the theory really theory in the scientific sense? Or is it not, on the contrary, a simple transposition into theory of the methodology of the practice (the cure)? Hence the very common modern view that beneath its theoretical exterior (which we owe to worthy but vain pretensions of Freud himself), psycho-analysis remains a mere practice that does sometimes give results, but not always; a mere practice extended into a technique (rules of analytic method), but *without a theory*, at least without a true theory: what it calls theory being merely the blind technical concepts in which it reflects the rules of its practice; a mere practice without theory . . . perhaps then, even simply a kind of magic? that succeeds, like all magic, because of its prestige – and its prestige, applied to the fulfilment of a social need or demand, therefore its only justification, its real justification. Lévi-Strauss would then have theorized this *magic*, this *social* practice, psycho-analysis, by pointing out the *shaman* as the ancestor of Freud.

A practice pregnant with a half-silent theory? A practice proud or ashamed to be merely the social magic of modern times? What then is psychoanalysis?

I

Lacan's first word is to say: in principle, Freud founded a *science*. A new science which was the science of a new object: the unconscious.

A rigorous statement. If psycho-analysis is a science because it is the science of a distinct object, it is also a science with the structure of all sciences: it has a *theory* and a *technique* (method) that make possible the knowledge and transformation of its object in a specific *practice*. As in every authentically constituted science, the practice is not the absolute of the science but a theoretically subordinate moment; the moment in which the theory, having become method (technique), comes into theoretical contact (knowledge) or practical contact (cure) with its specific object (the unconscious).

If this thesis is correct, analytical practice (the cure), which absorbs all the attention of those interpreters and philosophers eager for the intimacy of the confidential couple in which avowed sickness and professional medical secrecy exchange the sacred promises of intersubjectivity, does not contain the secrets of psycho-analysis; it only contains one part of the reality of psycho-analysis, the part which exists in the practice. It does not contain its theoretical secrets. If this thesis is correct, neither do the technique and method contain the secrets of psycho-analysis, except as every method does, by delegation, not from the practice but from the theory. Only the theory contains them, as in every scientific discipline.

In a hundred places in his work, Freud calls himself a theoretician; he compares psycho-analysis, as far as its scientificity is concerned, with the physical sciences that stem from Galileo, he repeats that the practice (cure) and analytical technique (analytical method) are only authentic because they are based on a scientific *theory*. Freud says time and again that a practice and a technique, even if they give results, do not deserve the name of science unless a theory gives them the right to it, not by mere declaration, but by rigorous proof.

Lacan's first word is to take these words literally. And to draw the conclusion: a return to Freud to seek out, distinguish and pin-point in him the theory from which all the rest, both practical and technical, stems by right.

A return to Freud. Why this new return to the source?

Lacan does not return to Freud as Husserl does to Galileo or Thales, to capture a birth at its birth – i.e. to achieve that religious philosophical preconception, purity, which like all water bubbling up out of the ground, is only pure at the very instant, the pure instant of its birth, in the pure passage from non-science to science. For Lacan, this passage is not pure, it is still impure: purity comes after the still 'muddy' passage (the invisible mud of its past suspended in the new-born water which pretends transparency, i.e. innocence). A return to Freud means: a return to the theory established, fixed and founded firmly in Freud himself, to the mature, reflected, supported and verified theory, to the advanced theory that has settled down in life (including practical life) to build its home, produce its method and give birth to its practice. The return to Freud is not a return to Freud's birth: but a return to his *maturity*. Freud's youth, the moving passage from not-yet-science to science (the period of the relations with Charcot, Bernheim, Breuer, up to the *Studies in Hysteria* – 1895) may indeed be of interest to us, but on a quite different level: as an example of the archaeology of a science – or as a negative index of immaturity, thereby precisely dating maturity and its arrival. The youth of a science is its prime of life; before this age it is old, its age the age of the preconceptions by which it lives, as a child does the preconceptions and hence the age of its parents.

That a young, and hence mature theory can relapse into childhood, i.e. into the preconceptions of its elders and their descendants, is proved by the whole history of psycho-analysis. This is the deeper meaning of the return to Freud proclaimed by Lacan. We must return to Freud to return to the maturity of Freudian theory, not to its childhood, but to its prime, which is its true youth – we must return to Freud beyond the theoretical childishness, the relapse into childhood in which all or a part of contemporary psycho-analysis, particularly in America, savours the advantages of surrender.

This relapse into childhood has a name that phenomenologists will understand straight away: psychologism – or another that Marxists will understand straight away: pragmatism. The modern history of psycho-analysis illustrates Lacan's judgement. Western Reason (legal, religious, moral and political *as well as* scientific) will only agree to conclude a pact of peaceful coexistence with psycho-analysis after years of non-recognition, contempt and insults – means that are still available anyway if all else fails – on condition of annexing it to its own sciences or myths: to psychology, whether behaviourist (Dalbiez), phenomenological (Merleau-Ponty) or existentialist (Sartre); to a more or less Jacksonian bio-neurology (Ey); to 'sociology' of the 'culturalist' or 'anthropological' type (dominant in the USA: Kardiner, Margaret Mead, etc); and to philosophy (cf. Sartre's 'existentialist psychoanalysis', Binswanger's '*Daseinanalyse*', etc.). To these confusions, to this mythologization of psycho-analysis, a discipline officially recognized at the price of compromise alliances sealed with *imaginary* ties of adoption but very real powers, some psycho-analysts have subscribed, only too happy to emerge at last from their theoretical ghetto, to be 'recognized' as full members of the great family of psychology, neurology, psychiatry, medicine, sociology, anthropology, philosophy – only too happy to certify their practical success with this 'theoretical' recognition which at last, after decades of insults and exile, confers on them citizen's rights in the world: the world of science, medicine and philosophy. They were not alerted to the suspicious side of this agreement, believing that the world was coming round to their positions – when they were themselves, with these honours, coming round to the world's positions – preferring its honours to its insults.

They thereby forgot that a science is only a science if it can claim a right to an object *of its own* – an object that is its own and its own *only* – not a mere foothold in an object loaned, conceded or abandoned by another science, one of the latter's 'aspects', the *leavings* that can be rehashed in the kitchen once the master of the house has eaten his fill. Concretely, if the whole of psycho-analysis is reduced to behaviourist or Pavlovian 'conditioning' in early childhood; if it is reduced to a dialectic of the *stages* which Freud's terminology designates as oral, anal and genital, latency and puberty; if, finally, it is reduced to the primitive experience of the Hegelian struggle, of the phenomenological for-others, or of the Heideggerian 'gulf' of being; if all psycho-analysis is merely this art of assimilating the leavings of neurology, biology, psychology, anthropology and philosophy, what can it claim as its specific object, what really distinguishes it from these disciplines and makes it in the full sense a science?[2]

2. The most dangerous of these temptations are those of *philosophy* (which gladly reduces the whole of the psycho-analysis to the dual experience of the cure and thereby 'verifies' the themes of phenomenological intersubjectivity, of the existence-project, or more generally of personalism); of *psychology* which appropriates most of the categories of psycho-analysis as so many attributes of a 'subject' in which, manifestly, it sees no problem; finally, of sociology which comes to the aid of psychology by providing it with an objective content for the 'reality principle' (social and familial imperatives) which the 'subject' need only 'internalize' to be armed with a 'super-ego' and the corresponding categories. Thus subordinated to psychology or sociology psycho-analysis is usually reduced to a technique of 'emotional' or 'affective' re-adaptation, or to a re-education of the 'relational function', neither of which have anything to do with its real object – but which unfortunately respond to a major demand, and what is more, to a demand that is highly tendentious in the contemporary world. Through this bias, psycho-analysis has become an article of mass consumption in modern culture, i.e. in modern ideology.

It is here that Lacan intervenes: he defends the irreducibility of analysis against these 'reductions' and deviations, which dominate most contemporary theoretical interpretations; he defends its irreducibility, which means *the irreducibility of its object*. That this defence requires an uncommon lucidity and firmness, sufficient to repulse all the voraciously hospitable assaults of the disciplines I have listed, cannot be doubted by anyone who has ever in his life measured the need for security (theoretical, moral, social and economic), i.e. the uneasiness, of corporations (whose status is indissolubly scientific-professional-legal-economic) whose balance and comfort is threatened by the appearance of a unique discipline that forces them all to re-investigate not only their own disciplines but the reasons why they believe in them, i.e. to doubt them, by the appearance of a science which, however little it is believed, threatens to violate the existing frontiers and hence to alter the *status quo* of several disciplines. Hence the contained passion and passionate contention of Lacan's language, unable to live or survive except in a state of alert and accusation: the language of a man of the besieged vanguard, condemned by the crushing strength of the threatened structures and corporations to forestall their blows, or at least to feint a response to them before they are delivered, thus discouraging the opponents from crushing him beneath their assault. Hence also the often paradoxical resort to the security provided by philosophies completely foreign to his scientific undertaking (Hegel, Heidegger), as so many intimidating witnesses thrown in the faces of part of his audience to retain their respect; and as so many witnesses to a possible objectivity, the natural ally of his thought, to reassure or educate the rest. As this resort was almost indispensable to sustain a discourse addressed *from within* to the medical profession alone, one would have to ignore both the conceptual weakness of medical studies in general and the profound need for theory felt by the best medical men, to condemn it out of hand. And since I am dealing with his language, the language which is the sum total of his prestige for some of the audience ('the Góngora of psycho-analysis', 'the Grand Dragon', the great officiant of an esoteric cult in which gesture, hushedness and solemnity can constitute the ritual of a real communication – or of a quite 'Parisian' fascination) – and for the rest (above all scientists or philosophers) his 'artifice', his strangeness and his 'hermeticism', it is clear that it bears some relation to the conditions of his practice as a teacher: since he has to teach the theory of the unconscious to doctors, analysts or analysands, in the rhetoric of his speech Lacan provides them with a dumbshow equivalent of the language of the unconscious (which, as is well known, is in its ultimate essence *'Witz'*, successful or unsuccessful pun and metaphor): the equivalent of the lived experience of their practice, whether as analyst or as analysand.

An understanding of this language's ideological and educational preconditions – i.e. the ability to maintain the distance of historical and theoretical 'exteriority' from its pedagogic 'interiority' – is enough to let us discern its objective meaning and scope – and recognize its basic proposal: to give Freud's discovery its measure in theoretical concepts by defining as rigorously as is possible today the *unconscious* and its 'laws', its whole object.

2

What is the *object* of psycho-analysis? It is *what* analytical technique deals with in the analytical practice of the cure, i.e. not the cure itself, not that supposedly dual system which is tailor-made for any phenomenology or morality –

but the '*effects*', prolonged into the surviving adult, of the extraordinary adventure which from birth to the liquidation of the Oedipal phase transforms a small animal conceived by a man and a woman into a small human child.

One of the 'effects' of the humanization of the small biological creature that results from human parturition: there in its place is the object of psycho-analysis, an object which has a simple name: '*the unconscious*'.

That this small biological being survives, and not as a 'wolf-child', that has become a little wolf or bear (as displayed in the princely courts of the eighteenth century), but as a *human child* (having escaped all childhood deaths, many of which are human deaths, deaths punishing the failure of humanization), that is the test all adult men have passed: they are the *never forgetful* witnesses, and very often the victims, of this victory, bearing in their most hidden, i.e. in their most clamorous parts, the wounds, weaknesses and stiffnesses that result from this struggle for human life or death. Some, the majority, have emerged more or less unscathed – or at least, give this out to be the case; many of these veretans bear the marks throughout their lives; some will die from their fight, though at some remove, the old wounds suddenly opening again in psychotic explosion, in madness, the ultimate compulsion of a 'negative therapeutic reaction'; others, more numerous, as 'normally' as you like, in the guise of an 'organic' decay. Humanity only inscribes its official deaths on its war memorials: those who were able to die on time, i.e. late, as men, in human wars in which only *human* wolves and gods tear and sacrifice one another. In its sole survivors, psycho-analysis is concerned with another struggle, with the only war without memoirs or memorials, the war humanity pretends it has never declared, the war it always thinks it has won in advance, simply because humanity is nothing but surviving this war, living and bearing children as culture in human culture: a war which is continually declared in each of its sons, who, projected, deformed and rejected, are required, each by himself in solitude and against death, to take the long forced march which makes mammiferous larvae into human children, *masculine* or *feminine subjects*.

This object is no business of the biologist's: this story is certainly not biological! – since from the beginning it is completely dominated by the constraint of the sexed human order that each mother engraves on the small human animal in maternal 'love' or hatred, starting from its alimentary rhythm and training. History, 'sociology' or anthropology have no business here, and this is no surprise for they deal with society and therefore with culture, i.e. with what is no longer this small animal – which only becomes human-sexual by crossing the infinite divide that separates life from humanity, the biological from the historical, 'nature' from 'culture'. Psychology is lost here, and this is hardly strange for it thinks that in its 'object' it is dealing with some *human* 'nature' or 'non-nature', with the genesis of this existent, identified and certified by culture itself (by the human) – when the object of psycho-analysis is the question with absolute priority, whether to be born or not to be (*naître ou n'être pas*), the aleatory abyss of the human-sexual itself in every human scion. Here 'philosophy' loses its bearings and its cover ('*repères*' and '*repaires*'), naturally! – for these unique origins rob it of the only origins it renders homage to for its existence: God, reason, consciousness, history and culture. It is clear that the object of psycho-analysis may be specific and that the modality of its material as well as the specificity of its 'mechanisms' (to use one of Freud's terms) are of quite another kind than the material and 'mechanisms' which are known to the biologist, the neurologist, the anthropologist, the sociologist, the psychologist and the philosopher. We need only recognize this specificity and hence the distinctness of the object that it derives from, in order to recognize the radical right of psycho-analysis to a specificity of its concepts in line with the specifiicity of its object: the unconcious and its effects.

3

Lacan would be the first to admit that his attempted theorization would have been impossible were it not for the emergence of a new science: *linguistics*. It is in the nature of the history of the sciences that one science may often not become a science except by recourse to a detour through other sciences, not only sciences that existed at its baptism but also some new late-comer among sciences that needed time before it could be born. The temporary opacity of the shadow cast on Freudian theory by the model of Helmholtz and Maxwell's thermodynamic physics has been dispersed today by the light that structural linguistics throws on it object, making possible an intelligible approach to that object. Freud himself said that everything depended on language. Lacan makes this more precise: 'the discourse of the unconscious is structured like a language'. In his first great work *The Interpretation of Dreams* (which is not anecdotal and superficial as is frequently suggested, but fundamental), Freud studied the 'mechanisms' and 'laws' of dreams, reducing their variants to two: *displacement* and *condensation*. Lacan recognized these as two essential figures of speech, called in linguistics metonymy and metaphor. Hence slips, failures, jokes and symptoms, like the elements of dreams themselves, became *signifiers*, inscribed in the chain of an unconscious discourse, doubling silently, i.e. deafeningly, in the misrecognition of 'repression', the chain of the human subject's verbal discourse. Hence we were introduced to the paradox, formally familiar to linguistics, of a double yet single discourse, unconscious yet verbal, having for its double field only a single field, with no beyond except in itself: the field of the 'Signifying Chain'. Hence the most important acquisitions of de Saussure and of the linguistics that descends from him began to play a justified part in the understanding of the process of the unconscious as well as that of the verbal discourse of the subject and of their inter-relationship, i.e. of their identical relation and non-relation in other words, of their reduplication and dislocation (*décalage*). Thereby philosophico-idealist interpretations of the unconscious as a second consciousness, of the unconscious as bad faith (Sartre), of the unconscious as the cankerous survival of a non-current structure or non-sense (Merleau-Ponty), all the interpretations of the unconscious as a biologico-archetypical 'id' (Jung) became what they were: not the beginnings of a theory but null 'theories', ideological misunderstandings.

It remained to define (I am forced into the crudest schematism, but how could I avoid it in such a short article?) the meaning of this *primacy* of the formal structure of language and its 'mechanisms' as they are encountered in the practice of analytical interpretation, as a function of the very foundations of this practice: its object, i.e. the 'effects' still present in the survivors of the forced 'humanization' of the small human animal into a *man* or a *woman*. This question cannot be answered merely by invoking the factual primacy of language as the sole object and means of analytical practice. Everything that happens in the cure does take place in and through language (including silence, its rhythms and scansions). But it is necessary to show *why* and *how* in principle the factual role of language in the cure as both raw material of analytic practice and means of production of its effects (the passage, as Lacan puts it, from an 'empty speech' to a 'full speech'), is only founded in fact in analytical practice because it is founded in *principle* in its object, the object that, in the last analysis, founds this practice and its technique: hence, since it is a science, in the *theory* of its object.

Herein no doubt lies the most original aspect of Lacan's work, his discovery. Lacan has shown that this transition from (ultimately purely) biological existence to human existence (the human child) is achieved within the Law of Order, the law I shall call the Law of Culture, and that this Law of Order is confounded in its *formal* essence with the order of language. What are we to understand by this formula, at first sight so enigmatic? Firstly, that the *whole of this transition* can only be grasped in terms of a recurrent language, as designated by the language of the adult or child in a *cure situation*, designated, assigned and localized within the law of language in which is established and presented all human order, i.e. every human role. Secondly, that in this assignment by the language of the cure appears the current, constant presence of the absolute effectiveness of order in the transition itself, of the Law of Culture in humanization.

To give some idea of this in a very few words, I shall indicate the two great moments of this *transition*. 1. The moment of the dual pre-Oedipal intercourse, in which the child, concerned with nothing but one alter-ego, the mother, who punctuates its life by her presence (*da!*) and absence (*fort!*),[3] lives this dual intercourse in the mode of the imaginary fascination of the ego, being itself *that* other, *any*

3. These are the two German expressions made famous by Freud, with which a small child under his observation sanctioned the appearance and disappearance of its mother by the manipulation of an arbitrary object that 'represented' her: a cotton-reel.

other, *every* other, all *the others* of primary narcissistic
identification, never able to take up the objectifying distance
of the third *vis-à-vis* either the other or itself; 2. the Oedipal
moment, in which a ternary structure emerges against the
background of the dual structure, when the third (the
father) intrudes on the imaginary satisfaction of dual
fascination, overthrows its economy, destroys its fascinations, and introduces the child to what Lacan calls the
Symbolic Order, the order of objectifying language that
will finally allow him to say: I, you, he, she or it, that will
therefore allow the small child to situate itself as a *human
child* in a world of adult thirds.

Hence two great moments: 1. that of the imaginary (pre-
Oedipal); 2. that of the symbolic (Oedipal resolution), or,
to use a different language, that of objectivity recognized in
its (symbolic) use, but not yet known (the knowledge of
objectivity arising at a quite different 'age' and also from a
quite different practice).

And the crucial point that Lacan has illuminated is this:
these two moments are dominated, governed and marked
by a single Law, the *Law of the Symbolic*. Even the moment
of the imaginary, which, for clarity's sake, I have just
presented as *preceding* the symbolic, as distinct from it –
hence as the first moment in which the child *lives* its immediate intercourse with a human being (its mother)
without recognizing it practically as the symbolic intercourse it is (i.e. as the intercourse of a small human child
with a human mother) – *is marked and structured in its
dialectic by the dialectic of the Symbolic Order itself*, i.e. by
the dialectic of human Order, of the human norm (the
norms of the temporal rhythms of feeding, hygiene, behaviour, of the concrete attitudes of recognition – the child's
acceptance, rejection, yes and no being merely the small
change, the *empirical* modalities of this constitutive Order,

the Order of Law and of the Right of attributory or exclus-
ory assignment), in the form of the Order of the signifier
itself, i.e., in the form of an Order *formally* identical with
the order of language.[4]

Where a superficial or prejudiced reading of Freud has
only seen happy, lawless childhood, the paradise of 'poly-
morphous perversity', a kind of state of nature only punct-
uated by stages of a biological type linked with the func-
tional primacy of some part of the human body, the site of a
'vital' need (oral, anal, genital),[5] Lacan demonstrates the
effectiveness of the Order, the Law, that has been lying in
wait for each infant born since before his birth, and seizes
him before his first cry, assigning to him his place and role,
and hence his fixed destination. Each stage traversed by the
sexed infant is traversed in the realm of Law, of the codes of
human assignment, communication and non-communica-
tion; his 'satisfactions' bear the indelible and constitutive
mark of the Law, of the claims of human Law, that, like all

4. *Formally*: for the Law of Culture, which is first introduced as language
and whose first form is language, is not exhausted by language; its content is
the real kinship structures and the determinate ideological formations in
which the persons inscribed in these structures live their functions. It is not
enough to know that the Western family is patriarchal and exogamic (kinship
structures) – we must also work out the ideological formations that govern
paternity, maternity, conjugality and childhood: what are 'husband-and-
wife-being', 'father-being', 'mother-being' and 'child-being' in the modern
world? A mass of research remains to be done on these ideological formations.
This is a task for *historical materialism*.

5. A branch of neuro-biology and one of psychology have been only too
pleased to discover in Freud a theory of 'stages', and they have not hesitated
to translate it directly and exhaustively into a theory of 'stadial growth', either
neuro-biological or bio-neuro-psychological – mechanically assigning to
neuro-biological growth the role of an 'essence' for which the Freudian
'stages' are merely the 'phenomena' pure and simple. This perspective is
nothing but a re-edition of the old theory of mechanical parallelism. This is
directed particularly towards the disciples of Wallon, for Wallon himself did
not take any notice of Freud.

law, cannot be 'ignored' by anyone, least of all by those
ignorant of it, but may be evaded or violated by everyone,
above all by its most faithful adherents. That is why any
reduction of childhood traumas to a balance of 'biological
frustrations' alone, is in principle erroneous, since the Law
that covers them, as a Law, abstracts from all contents,
exists and acts as a Law only in and by this abstraction, and
the infant submits to this rule and receives it from his first
breath.[6] This is the beginning, and has always been the
beginning, even where there is no living father, of the official
presence of the Father (who is Law), hence of the Order of
the human signifier, i.e. of the Law of Culture: this discourse, the absolute precondition of any discourse, this discourse present at the top, i.e. absent in the depths, in all
verbal discourse, the discourse of this Order, this discourse
of the Other, of the great Third, which is this Order itself:
the discourse of the unconscious. This gives us a hold, a
conceptual hold on the unconscious, which is in each human
being the absolute place where his particular discourse seeks
its own place, seeks, misses, and in missing, finds its own

6. There is a risk that the theoretical scope of this formal condition may be
misconstrued, if this is countered by citing the apparently biological concepts
(libido, affects, instincts, desire) in which Freud thinks the 'content' of the
unconscious. For example, when he says that the dream is a *'wish-fulfilment'*
(*Wunscherfüllung*). The sense here is the same as the sense in which Lacan
opposes man's 'empty speech' to his 'full speech', as to the language of
unconscious 'desire'. But only on the basis of this formal condition do these
(apparently biological) concepts obtain their authentic meaning, or can this
meaning be assigned and thought and a curative technique defined and
applied. Desire, the basic category of the unconscious, is only intelligible in
its specificity as the sole meaning of the discourse of the human subject's
unconscious: the meaning that emerges in and through the 'play' of the
signifying chain which makes up the discourse of the unconscious. As such,
'desire' is marked by the structure that commands human development. As
such, desire is radically distinct from organic and essentially biological 'need'.
There is no essential continuity between organic need and unconscious

place, its own anchor to its place, in the imposition, imposture, complicity and denegation of its own imaginary fascinations.

That in the Oedipal phase the sexed child becomes a sexual human child (man or woman) by testing its imaginary fantasms against the Symbolic, and if all 'goes well' finally becomes and accepts itself as what it is: a little boy or little girl among adults, with the rights of a child in this adult world, and, like all children, with the full *right* to become one day 'like daddy', i.e. a masculine human being with a wife (and no longer only a mother), or 'like mummy', i.e. a feminine human being with a husband (and not just a father) – these things are only the destination of the long forced march towards human childhood.

That all the material of this ultimate drama is provided by a previously formed language, which, in the Oedipal phase, is centred and arranged wholly around the signifier *phallus*: the emblem of the Father, the emblem of right, of the Law, the fantasy image of all Right – this may seem astonishing or arbitrary, but all psycho-analysts attest to it as a fact of experience.

---

desire, any more than there is between man's biological existence and his historical existence. Desire is determined in its ambiguous being (its 'failure-in-being' – *manque à être* – says Lacan) by the structure of the Order that imposes its mark on it and destines it for a placeless existence, the existence of repression, for its resources as well as for its disappointments. The specific reality of desire cannot be reached by way of organic need any more than the specific reality of historical existence can be reached by way of the biological existence of 'man'. On the contrary: just as it is the categories of history that allow us to define the specificity of man's historical existence, including some apparently purely biological determinations such as his 'needs' or demographic phenomena, by distinguishing his historical existence from a purely biological existence – similarly, it is the essential categories of the unconscious that allow us to grasp and define the very meaning of desire by distinguishing it from the biological realities that support it (exactly as biological existence supports historical existence) but neither *constitute*, nor *determine* it.

The last Oedipal stage, 'castration', shows us why. When the small boy lives and resolves the tragic and beneficial situation of castration, he accepts the fact that he *has not* the same Right (phallus) as his father, in particular, that he has not the same Right as his father over his mother, who is thereby revealed as endowed with the intolerable status of double use, mother for the small boy, wife for the father; but by accepting that he has not the same right as his father, he gains the assurance that one day, *later on*, when he grows up, he will get the right which is now refused him through his lack of 'means'. He has only a little right, which will grow big if he will grow big himself by taking care to 'mind his p's and q's' (*'manger sa soupe'*). For her part, when the little girl lives and assumes the tragic and beneficial situation of castration, she accepts that she has not the same right as her mother, and hence she doubly accepts that she has not the same right (phallus) as her father, since her mother has not this right (no phallus), although she is a woman, because she is a woman, and she simultaneously accepts that she has not the same right as her mother, i.e. that she is not yet a woman as her mother is. But she thereby gains in return her own small right: the right of a little girl, and the promise of a large right, the full right of a woman when she grows up, if she will grow up accepting the Law of Human Order, i.e. submitting to it if need be to deflect it – by not minding her p's and q's 'properly'.

In either case, whether it be the moment of dual fascination of the Imaginary (1) or the (Oedipal) moment of the lived recognition of the insertion into the Symbolic Order (2), the whole dialectic of the transition in all its essential details is stamped by the seal of Human Order, of the Symbolic, for which linguistics provides us with the *formal* laws, i.e. the *formal* concept.

Psycho-analytic theory can thus give us what makes each science no pure speculation but a science: the definition of the *formal* essence of its object, the precondition for any practical, technical application of it to its *concrete* objects. Thereby psycho-analytic theory escapes the classical idealist antinomies formulated by Politzer for example, when, while demanding of psycho-analysis (whose revolutionary theoretical scope he was the first in France to realize) that it be a science of the true 'concrete', a 'concrete psychology', he attacked it for its *abstractions*: the unconscious, the Oedipus complex, the castration complex, etc. How, said Politzer, can psycho-analysis claim to be the science of the *concrete* it aims to be and could be, if it persists in *abstractions* which are merely the 'concrete' alienated in an abstract and metaphysical psychology? How can one reach the 'concrete' from such abstractions, from the abstract? In fact, no science can do without abstraction, even when, in its 'practice' (which is not, NB, the theoretical practice of that science but the practice of its concrete *application*), it deals only with those peculiar and unique variants that constitute each individual 'drama'. As Lacan thinks them in Freud – and Lacan thinks nothing but Freud's concepts, giving them the form of our scientificity, the only scientificity there can be – the 'abstractions' of psycho-analysis are really the authentic scientific concepts of their object, insofar as, as concepts of their object, they contain within them the index, measure and basis for the necessity of their abstraction, i.e., the measure of their relation to the 'concrete', and hence of their specific relation to the concrete of their application, commonly called analytic practice (the cure).

So the Oedipal phase is not a hidden '*meaning*' which merely lacks consciousness or speech – it is not a structure buried in the past that can always be restructured or surpassed by 'reactivating its meaning'; the Oedipus complex is the dramatic structure, the 'theatrical machine'[7] imposed by the Law of Culture on every involuntary, conscripted candidate to humanity, a structure containing in itself not only the possibility of, but the necessity for the concrete variants in which it *exists*, for every individual who reaches its threshold, lives through it and survives it. In its application, in what is called its practice (the cure), psychoanalysis works on the concrete 'effects'[8] of these variants, i.e. on the modality of the specific and absolutely unique nexus in which the Oedipal transition was and is begun, completed, missed or eluded by some particular individual. These *variants* can be thought and known in their essence itself on the basis of the structure of the Oedipal *invariant*, precisely because this whole transition is marked from its beginnings in fascination, in its most 'aberrant' as well as in its most 'normal' forms, by the Law of this structure, the ultimate form of access to the Symbolic within the Law of the Symbolic itself.

I know that these brief suggestions will not only appear to be, but are, summary and schematic; that a number of notions put forward here require extended development if they are to be justified and established. Even if their wellfoundedness and the relations they bear to the set of notions that underly them were clarified, even if they were compared with the letter of Freud's analyses, they would pose their own problems in their turn: not only problems of

7. An expression of Lacan's ('*machine*'), referring to Freud ('*ein anderes Schauspiel*' . . . '*Schauplatz*'). From Politzer, who talks of 'drama' to Freud and Lacan who speak of theatre, stage, *mise en scène*, machinery, theatrical genre, *metteur en scène*, etc., there is all the distance between the spectator who takes himself for the theatre – and the theatre itself.

8. If this term 'effect' is examined in the context of a classical theory of causality, it reveals a conception of the continuing presence of the cause in its effects (cf. Spinoza).

conceptual formation, definition and clarification, but real, new problems, necessarily produced by the development of the work of theorization we have just discussed. For example, how can we rigorously formulate the relation between the *formal* structure of language, the absolute precondition for the existence and intelligibility of the unconscious, on the one hand, the concrete kinship structures on the other, and finally the concrete ideological formations in which the specific functions implied by the kinship structures (paternity, maternity, childhood) are lived? Is it conceivable that the historical variation of these latter structures (kinship, ideology) might materially affect some or other aspect of the instances isolated by Freud? Or again, to what extent may the simple definition of the object and location of Freud's discovery, rationally conceived, react on the disciplines from which it distinguished itself (such as psychology, social psychology, sociology), and raise for them questions as to the (often problematic) status of their objects? And selecting one more from among so many possible questions: what relations are there between analytic theory and 1. the historical preconditions of its appearance, and 2. the social preconditions of its application?

1. *Who*, then, *was Freud, simultaneously* the founder of analytic theory and the inaugurator, as Analyst number one, *self-analysed*, original Father, of the long line of practitioners who claim descent from him?

2. *Who*, then, *are the psycho-analysts*, who *simultaneously* (and as naturally as if it went without saying) accept Freudian theory, the didactic tradition that descends from Freud, and the social and economic conditions (the social status of their 'associations' which cling tightly to the status of *medical* corporations) under which they practice? To what extent do the historical origins and socio-economic con-

ditions of the practice of psycho-analysis react an analytical theory and technique? Most important of all, to what extent do the theoretical *silence* of psychoanalysts about these questions (for this is certainly the state of affairs) and the theoretical *repression* these problems meet with in the world of analysis, affect both analytic theory and analytical technique in their content itself? Cannot the eternal question of the 'end of analysis', among others, be related to this repression, i.e. to the *non-thoughtness of these problems* which derive from an epistemological history of psycho-analysis and a social (and ideological) history of the world of analysis?

Here are a number of real questions, really posed, and they constitute immediately an equal number of fields of research. It may be that in the near future certain notions will emerge transformed from this test.

And this test is rooted in the test Freud, in his own field, applied to a particular legal, ethical and philosophical, i.e. definitively ideological, image of 'man', of the human 'subject'. Not in vain did Freud somtiemes compare the critical reception of his discovery with the upheavals of the Copernican Revolution. Since Copernicus, we have known that the earth is not the 'centre' of the universe. Since Marx, we have known that the human subject, the economic, political or philosophical ego is not the 'centre' of history – and even, in opposition to the Philosophers of the Enlightenment and to Hegel, that history has no 'centre' but possesses a structure which has no necessary 'centre' except in ideological misrecognition. In turn, Freud has discovered for us that the real subject, the individual in his unique essence, has not the form of an ego, centred on the 'ego', on 'consciousness' or on 'existence' – whether this is the existence of the for-itself, of the body-proper or of 'behaviour' – that the human subject is de-centred, constituted by a structure which has no 'centre' either, except in the imaginary misrecognition of the 'ego', i.e. in the ideological formations in which it 'recognizes' itself.

It must be clear that this has opened up one of the ways which may perhaps lead us some day to a better understanding of this *structure of misrecognition*, which is of particular concern for all investigations into ideology.

January 1964 (corrected February 1969)

BIBLIOGRAPHICAL STUDY NOTE:

Access to Lacan's work will be facilitated if it is approached in the following order:

1. 'Les complexes familiaux en pathologie', *Encyclopédie Française*, de Monzie, Vol. 8: 'La vie mentale' (1938).
2. 'La causalité psychique', *Évolution Psychiatrique*, fasc. 1, 1947.
3. 'Le stade du miroir comme formateur de la fonction du Je', *Écrits*, Paris 1966, pp. 93-100 (English translation, *New Left Review* 51, Sept.-Oct. 1968).
4. 'La chose freudienne', *Écrits*, pp. 401-36.
5. 'Les formations de l'inconscient', Seminar 1958-59. *Bulletin de psychologie*.
6. 'Les relations d'objet et les structures freudiennes', Seminar 1956-57, *Bulletin de psychologie*, 10.
7. 'Le désir et son interprétation', Seminar 1958-59, *Bulletin de psychologie*, Jan. 1960.
8. 'Fonction et champ de la parole et du langage en psychanalyse', *Écrits*, pp. 237-322 (English translation with a commentary by Anthony Wilden as *The Language of the Self*, Johns Hopkins Press, Baltimore, 1968). 'Remarque sur le rapport de Daniel Lagache: "Psychanalyse et structure de la personalité" ', *Écrits*, pp. 647-84; 'La direction de la cure et les principes de son pouvoir', *Écrits*, pp. 585-646; 'L'instance de la lettre dans l'inconscient ou la raison depuis Freud', *Écrits*, pp. 493-528 (English translation, *Yale French Studies* 36-7, 1966, pp. 112-47); and other studies from the seven issues of the magazine *La Psychanalyse*.
9. Of texts written by Lacan's pupils or under his influence, the reader is advised to start with Serge Leclaire's articles in *La Psychanalyse*, Serge Leclaire and Jean Laplanche on the unconscious in *Les Temps Modernes*, July 1961, J. B. Lefèvre-Pontalis, 'Freud Aujourd'hui', *Les Temps Modernes*, 124-6 (1965), J. Laplanche's book on Hölderlin and Maud Mannoni: *L'enfant arriéré et sa mère*, 1963.

A Letter on Art
in Reply to André Daspre

La Nouvelle Critique has sent me your letter.[1] I hope you will permit me, if not to reply to all the questions it poses, at least to add a few comments to yours in the line of your own reflections.

First of all, you should know that I am perfectly conscious of the *very schematic* character of my article on Humanism.[2] As you have noticed, it has the disadvantage that it gives a 'broad' idea of ideology without going into the analysis of details. As it does not mention art, I realize that it is possible to wonder whether art should or should not be ranked as such among ideologies, to be precise, whether art and ideology are one and the same thing. That, I feel, is how you have been tempted to *interpret* my silence.

The problem of the relations between art and ideology is a very complicated and difficult one. However, I can tell you in what directions our investigations tend. *I do not rank real art among the ideologies*, although art does have a quite particular and specific relationship with ideology. If you would like some idea of the initial elements of this thesis and the very complicated developments it promises,

1. See *La Nouvelle Critique*, no. 175, April 1966, pp. 136–41.
2. *La Nouvelle Critique*, no. 164, March 1965; *For Marx*, pp. 242–7.

I advise you to read carefully the article Pierre Macherey has written on 'Lenin as a critic of Tolstoy' in *La Pensée*, No. 121, 1965.[3] Of course, that article is only a beginning, but it does pose the problem of the relations between art and ideology and of the specificity of art. This is the direction in which we are working, and we hope to publish important studies on this subject in a few months time.

The article will also give you a first idea of the relationship between art and knowledge. Art (I mean authentic art, not works of an average or mediocre level) does not give us a *knowledge* in the *strict sense*, it therefore does not replace knowledge (in the modern sense: scentific knowledge), but what it gives us does nevertheless maintain a certain *specific relationship* with knowledge. This relationship is not one of identity but one of difference. Let me explain. I believe that the peculiarity of art is to 'make us see' (*nous donner à voir*), 'make us perceive', 'make us feel' something which *alludes* to reality. If we take the case of the novel, Balzac or Solzhenitsyn, as you refer to them, they make us *see*, *perceive* (but not *know*) something which *alludes* to reality.

It is essential to take the words which make up this first provisional definition literally if we are to avoid lapsing into an identification of what art gives us and what science gives us. What art makes us *see*, and therefore gives to us in the form of *'seeing'*, *'perceiving'* and *'feeling'* (which is not the form of *knowing*), is the *ideology* from which it is born, in which it bathes, from which it detaches itself as art and to which it *alludes*. Macherey has shown this very clearly in the case of Tolstoy, by extending Lenin's analyses. Balzac and Solzhenitsyn give us a 'view' of the ideology to which their work alludes and with which it is constantly fed, a view which presupposes a *retreat*, an *internal distantiation*

3. Now in Pierre Macherey, *Pour une théorie de la production littéraire*, Paris, 1966, pp. 125–57.

from the very ideology from which their novels emerged. They make us 'perceive' (but not know) in some sense *from the inside*, by an *internal distance*, the very ideology in which they are held.

These distinctions, which are not just shades of meaning but specific differences, should *in principle* enable us to resolve a number of problems.

First the problem of the 'relations' between art and science. Neither Balzac nor Solzhenitsyn gives us any *knowledge* of the world they describe, they only make us 'see', 'perceive' or 'feel' the reality of the ideology of that world. When we speak of ideology we should know that ideology slides into all human activity, that it is identical with the 'lived' experience of human existence itself: that is why the form in which we are 'made to see' ideology in great novels has as its content the 'lived' experience of individuals. This 'lived' experience is not a *given*, given by a pure 'reality', but the spontaneous 'lived experience' of ideology in its peculiar relationship to the real. This is an important comment, for it enables us to understand that art does not deal with a reality *peculiar to itself*, with a *peculiar domain* of reality in which it has a monopoly (as you tend to imply when you write that 'with art, knowledge becomes human', that the object of art is 'the individual'), whereas science deals with a *different domain* of reality (say, in opposition to 'lived experience' and the 'individual', the abstraction of structures). Ideology is also an object of science, the 'lived experience' is also an object of science, the 'individual' is also an object of science. The real difference between art and science lies in the *specific form* in which they give us the same object in quite different ways: art in the form of 'seeing' and 'perceiving' or 'feeling', science in the form of *knowledge* (in the strict sense, by concepts).

The same thing can be said in other terms. If Solzhenitsyn does 'make us see' the 'lived experience' (in the sense defined earlier) of the 'cult of personality' and its effects, in no way does he give us a *knowledge* of them: this knowledge is the conceptual knowledge of the complex mechanisms which eventually produce the 'lived experience' that Solzhenitsyn's novel discusses. If I wanted to use Spinoza's language again here, I could say that art makes us 'see' 'conclusions without premises', whereas knowledge makes us penetrate into the mechanism which produces the 'conclusions' out of the 'premises'. This is an important distinction, for it enables us to understand that a novel on the 'cult', however profound, may draw attention to its 'lived' effects, but *cannot give an understanding of it*; it may put the question of the 'cult' on the agenda, but it cannot *define the means* which will make it possible to remedy these effects.

In the same way, these few elementary principles perhaps enable us to point the direction from which we can hope for an answer to another question you pose: how is it that Balzac, despite his personal political options, 'makes us see' the 'lived experience' of capitalist society in a critical form? I dó not believe one can say, as you do, that he *'was forced by the logic of his art to abandon certain of his political conceptions in his work as a novelist'*. On the contrary, we know that Balzac *never abandoned* his political positions. We know even more: his peculiar, reactionary political positions played a decisive part in the production of the content of his work. This is certainly a paradox, but it is the case, and history provides us with a number of examples to which Marx drew our attention (on Balzac, I refer you to the article by R. Fayolle in the special 1965 number of *Europe*). These are examples of a deformation of sense very commonly found in the dialectic of ideologies. See what Lenin says about Tolstoy (cf. Macherey's article): Tolstoy's personal ideological position is one component of the deep-lying causes of the *content* of his work. The fact that the content of the work of Balzac and Tolstoy is 'detached' from their political ideology and in some way makes us 'see' it from the *outside*, makes us 'perceive' it by a distantiation inside that ideology, *presupposes that ideology itself*. It is certainly possible to say that it is an 'effect' of *their art* as novelists that it produces this distance inside their ideology, which makes us 'perceive' it, but it is not possible to say, as you do, that art *'has its own logic'* which *'made Balzac abandon his political conceptions'*. On the contrary, *only because he retained them could he produce his work*, only because he stuck to his political ideology could he produce *in it* this internal 'distance' which gives us a critical 'view' of it.

As you see, in order to answer most of the questions posed for us by the existence and specific nature of art, we are forced to produce an adequate (scientific) *knowledge* of the processes which produce the 'aesthetic effect' of a work of art. In other words, in order to answer the question of the relationship between art and knowledge we must produce a *knowledge of art*.

You are conscious of this necessity. But you ought also to know that in this issue we still have a long way to go. The *recognition* (even the political recognition) of the existence and importance of art does not constitute *a knowledge of art*. I do not even think that it is possible to take as the beginnings of knowledge the texts you refer to,[4] or even Joliot-Curie, quoted by Marcenac.[5] To say a few words about the sentence attributed to Joliot-Curie, it contains a terminology

4. [Jean Marcenac, Elsa Triolet, Lukács, among others.
5. [Jean Marcenac, *Les Lettres Françaises*, 1966. 'I have always regretted the fact that F. Joliot-Curie never pursued the project he suggested to me at the time of Eluard's death, the project of a comparative study of poetic creation and scientific creation, which he thought might eventually prove an identity in their procedures.']

– 'aesthetic *creation*, scientific *creation*' – a terminology which is certainly quite common, but one which in my opinion must be *abandoned* and replaced by another, in order to be able to pose the problem of the knowledge of art in the proper way. I know that the artist, and the art lover, *spontaneously* express themselves in terms of 'creation', etc. It is a 'spontaneous' language, but we know from Marx and Lenin that every 'spontaneous' language is an *ideological* language, the vehicle of an ideology, here the ideology of art and of the activity productive of aesthetic effects. Like all knowledge, the knowledge of art presupposes a preliminary *rupture* with the language of *ideological spontaneity* and the constitution of a body of scientific concepts to replace it. It is essential to be conscious of the necessity for this rupture with ideology to be able to undertake the constitution of the edifice of a knowledge of art.

Here perhaps, is where I must express a sharp reservation about what you say. I am not perhaps speaking about exactly what you *want* or *would like* to say, but about what you *actually* do say. When you counterpose '*rigorous reflection on the concepts of Marxism*' to '*something else*', in particular to what art gives us, I believe you are establishing a comparison which is either incomplete or illegitimate. Since art in fact provides us with *something else* other than science, there is not an opposition between them, but a difference. On the contrary, if it is a matter of *knowing* art, it is absolutely essential to begin with '*rigorous reflection on the basic concepts of Marxism*': there is no other way. And when I say, '*it is essential to begin . . .*', it is not enough to *say* it, it is essential to *do* it. If not, it is easy to extricate oneself with a passing acknowledgement, like '*Althusser proposes to return to a rigorous study of Marxist theory. I agree that this is indispensable. But I do not believe that it is enough.*' My response to this is the only real criticism: there is a way of declaring an exigency 'indispensable' which consists precisely of *dispensing with it*, dispensing with a careful consideration of all its implications and consequences – by the acknowledgement accorded it in order to move quickly on to 'something else'. Now I believe that the only way we can hope to reach a real knowledge of art, to go deeper into the specificity of the work of art, to know the mechanisms which produce the 'aesthetic effect', is precisely to spend a long time and pay the greatest attention to the *'basic principles of Marxism'* and not to be in a hurry to 'move on to something else', for if we move on too quickly to 'something else' we shall arrive not at a *knowledge* of art, but at an *ideology* of art: e.g., at the latent humanist ideology which may be induced by what you say about the relations between art and the 'human', and about artistic 'creation', etc.

If we must turn (and this demands slow and arduous work) to the 'basic principles of Marxism' in order to be able to pose correctly, in concepts which are not the *ideological* concepts of aesthetic spontaneity, but *scientific* concepts adequate to their object, and thus necessarily *new* concepts, it is not in order to pass art silently by or to sacrifice it to science: it is quite simply in order to *know* it, and to give it its due.

April 1966

Other works by **Louis Althusser** available in Verso:

For Marx

For Marx includes Althusser's polemical reassessment of Marx's early writings, his celebrated essay on 'Contradiction and Overdetermination', a note on materialist theatre in Bertolazzi and Brecht and a critique of attempts to construct a 'Marxist humanism'.

An important revaluation of Marx's early writing
Tribune

Reading Capital

Reading Capital presents Louis Althusser's systematic theory of a Marxism cleansed of all idealist and Hegelian notions.

The strength of Althusser's objections to the Hegelian interpretation of Marx is substantial, the acuteness of his analysis of certain weaknesses of the thought of Gramsci and of Sartre is impressive, the critique of 'model-building' is to the point. . . . One reads his passionate study with attention, even with excitement.
Times Literary Supplement

Montesquieu, Rousseau, Marx

In the first two essays of this book, Louis Althusser analyses the work of two of the greatest thinkers of the Enlightenment, whose thought is still the focus of contemporary controversy – Montesquieu and Rousseau. The third essay examines Marx's relationship to Hegel and elaborates on the discussions of this theme in Althusser's earlier books.

This is a stimulating application of Marxist thinking in what for most English-speaking readers is likely to be unfamiliar territory.
'Morning Star'

Other titles of interest from Verso:

Marx and Human Nature: Refutation of a Legend

Norman Geras

'Marx did not reject the idea of a human nature. He was right not to do so.' That is the conclusion of this passionate and polemical new work by Norman Geras. The belief that Marx's historical materialism entails a denial of the conception of human nature has been shored up by recent Althusserian writing. 'Because this fixation still exists and is misguided, it is still necessary to challenge it.' Thus begins Geras's assault on those who try to deny that there are real basic needs and capacities inherent in human nature.

From Luther to Popper: Studies in Critical Philosophy

Herbert Marcuse

This is the first paperback edition of what is now generally recognized as being among Marcuse's most important writings on philosophy. Taking a critique of Martin Luther as his starting point, Marcuse proceeds via a series of astringent investigations of Kant, Burke, Hegel and Bergson, to extended studies of Marx's *Philosophical and Economic Manuscripts*, Sartre's *Being and Nothingness*, and Karl Popper's *The Poverty of Historicism*.

'The critique of Karl Popper is excellent and the critical account of Sartre's early existentialism is the most able and acute short comment I have ever read on the subject.'

The New Statesman

In The Tracks of Historical Materialism

Perry Anderson

What have been the major changes in the intellectual landscape of the Left since the mid-seventies? Have they on balance represented an emancipation or a retreat for socialist culture as a whole? *In The Tracks of Historical Materialism* looks at some of the paradoxes in the evolution of Marxist thought in this period, spanning a broad field from history to economics, politics to literature, sociology to philosophy.

'Anderson's work is distinguished not only by its theoretical brilliance but by its moral conscientiousness.'

Terry Eagleton in Economy and Society

Two important works by **Sartre** published by Verso:

Critique of Dialectical Reason

Jean-Paul Sartre

At the height of the Algerian War, Jean-Paul Sartre embarked on a fundamental reappraisal of his own philosophical and political thought. The result was the *Critique de la Raison Dialectique*, in which he set out the basic categories for a renovated theory of history that he believed was necessary for post-war Marxism. This is the essential counterpart and criticism of his earlier *Being and Nothingness*.

'A landmark in modern social thought . . . A turning-point in the thinking of our time.'

Guardian

Between Existentialism and Marxism

Jean-Paul Sartre

The essays and interviews collected here, for the first time in paperback, are a vivid demonstration of the range of Sartre's interests, part of his attempt to combine his original existentialism to a rethought Marxism. A long and brilliant autobiographical interview, given to *New Left Review* in 1969, constitutes the best single overview of his whole career. Writings on the Vietnam War, the invasion of Czechoslovakia in 1968 and the May 1968 revolt in France; essays on Kierkegaard, Mallarmé and Tintoretto; an assessment of Freudian psychoanalysis, and a critical reflection on the role of intellectuals in advanced capitalism: these are the subjects that reveal Sartre's exuberant intelligence in memorable form on every occasion.

'Sartre retains his full power to challenge: not just in the conventional sense but in a way that makes clear what intellectual challenge really is.'

Raymond Williams